SANTONA PUBLICATIONS
2009

BUILDING MICRO-LAYOUTS

Design tips, techniques and project plans

by
PAUL A. LUNN

BUILDING MICRO-LAYOUTS

First published in 2009
ISBN 978-1-907094-20-0

British Library Cataloguing in Publication Data. A catalogue record for this book is available from the British Library.

Published by: Santona Publications, 382 Carlton Hill, Carlton, Nottingham. NG4 1JA. Santona Publications is an imprint of Book Law Publications, 382 Carlton Hill, Carlton, Nottingham. NG4 1JA.

Printed by the Amadeus Press, West Yorkshire.
Additional information by Steve Flint.
Layout designs and watercolour impressions by the author.
Book design and graphics (from the author's originals) by Steve Flint.
Photographs, unless otherwise credited, by the author and Steve Flint courtesy Railway Modeller.
The author and publisher acknowledge the support of Peco Publications and Publicity in the preparation of this book.

Front cover: Shell Island, a classic micro-layout built by Neil Rushby.
Title page: a scene on Dave Tailby's Saxlingham, a truncated East Anglian branch built in the micro-layout idiom.

Contents

Part one. Micro-layouts and how to build them

Part two. Planning a mic

Part three. A gallery of ins

Part four. Plans, themes an es

Errata — Page 3: contents list.

About the plans in this book

All plans have been drawn to scale using imperial units. Each square on the grid backgrounds represents 1 sq. ft. Track is represented by either two rails and sleepers, two rails only, or just a single rule, depending on the size and scale of the plan. Although every attempt as been made to produce the plans as accurately as possible, absolute scale cannot be guaranteed and anyone contemplating building one of them is strongly recommended to carry out their own viability checks with track templates or actual track parts beforehand.

About the author

Paul's grandfather was a ganger on the London and North Eastern and ultimately British Railways between Leeds and Wakefield in West Yorkshire. His mother was a porter at Outwood Station just after the war and his uncle, after serving time as a fireman and driver, became shed foreman at Healey Mills. School holidays were spent at his grandparents' family home and it was here that Paul established himself as a model maker. Inspired by the fast Leeds to London expresses, the grimy freights outside his bedroom window and Lofthouse Colliery with its motley collection of locos and wagons, it was no wonder that railways, both real and model, would have a lasting impact.

As a hobby, the first step into railway model journalism came way back in 1984 and since then Paul has been a regular contributor to several of the monthly magazines. In 2003 he was a joint author on the best selling Santona Publications' title: Model Railway Design and Planning Handbook. More recently, in 2005 he was invited by Peco to create a new OO/HO Setrack Planbook. Paul is now self-employed and his business, Writeline, run by himself and his wife Anne, is best described as providing creative images and text on model and prototype railway subjects.

It's surprising that Paul never worked for the national railway, considering his interest in the topic: he settled instead on a career in art and working with people with a learning disability. However, never one to miss a chance here you see him driving Peak Rails' 0-6-0 austerity saddle tank in War Department guise.

Introduction

Micro-layout is an American term used to describe an exceptionally small layout and whilst I'm generally not in favour of yet another 'Americanism' it is in my mind more appropriate than its British equivalent – the Cameo. A cameo can be many things; it's a particularly dated word not so comfortable in today's language and certainly not as succinct as micro-layout.

What is a micro-layout? I suspect it means different things to different people but feel particularly comfortable with Roy Links' suggestion, Railway Modeller October 1978, "that it's a subtle blend of the diorama (essentially static) and a working layout (often too large)" and few of us could disagree when Iain Rice said that a micro-layout is "certainly more satisfying than no layout at all", Modelling Railways Illustrated, volume 3.

Early examples and especially those published at that time fall into what I call track-on-a-plank layouts. Limitations were obviously time, space and funding but perhaps less obvious, though with hindsight, was a lack of imagination. There were of course a number of notable exceptions like Andrew Knight's Yarmouth Quay, which is one of several at the heart of today's more sophisticated micro-layouts. In all fairness, layouts of all sizes have become more sophisticated as modellers strive for greater realism, but nowhere is this more noticeable than in the micro-layout. Michael Andress, quoting Cyril Freezer in Baseboards, Track and Electrification – PSL Railway Guide, said, "It's easier to build a good small than a good large layout," and Iain Rice was not alone in this thought when he suggested that, "A small slice of excellence…may be more desirable than a plateful of plain pudding." Modelling Railways Illustrated, volume 1.

The table on page 7 undoubtedly proves that micro-layouts almost certainly came about as a direct result of a change in people's circumstances and over recent years interest in them has grown to the point where examples feature regularly both at exhibition and within the model railway press. It's been my experience that small layouts like Walker Marine cause a considerable stir when on public view and are extremely productive in promoting the well being of all model railways. That said, it's fair to say this success has not been without its critics, citing that trains have nowhere to run or that scale accuracy has been compromised in order to fit a minimum space. Like all transitional periods, when new ideas are steadily creeping in, it will take time for micro-layouts to be accepted in their own right and as an essential part of mainstream modelling with much to contribute.

Modellers continue to build micro-layouts worldwide, with a particularly strong movement in the U.S. and an emerging one in the U.K. Whilst the essential reasoning remains the same around space, time and cost, I do believe that in more recent times the very basic make up of micro-layouts has started to change. Many people are building layouts this way not because of any imposition but because its fun, there's great opportunity, flexibility and variety and perhaps most important of all, there's the challenge; will it work and will it look right, will it all fit in? Brian J. Taylor with *Snailspeed*, Railway Modeller July 1993, proved, "It is surprising what you can do in a fairly small space. *Snailspeed* is only 4' x 1' 10" and has two stations, part of a harbour, twenty two buildings and a number of sidings for both standard and narrow gauges." I would add that there is no evidence of overcrowding in a model that is, to say the least, quite stunning.

Considering the benefits of micro-layout modelling, described in more detail further on, it's clear as to why you should consider this medium. What I have endeavoured to undertake in the course of my ramblings is to show you how to achieve satisfying results through planning, design and production.

None of this would have been possible without the truly inspirational influence of Chris Ellis, Cyril Freezer, Carl Arendt and the support and opportunities provided by Steve Flint and Michael Pritchard of Railway Modeller.

A word of warning. Cyril once said, designing layouts can be fun, but it can lead to problems. One reason his own layouts tend to have rather short lives is that he has all too often, drawn up a variant to fit a site and found the lure of a fresh design too great. How true Cyril… how true?

Paul A. Lunn
Chesterfield 2008

WHY BUILD A MICRO-LAYOUT?

During the months I was preparing this book, letters appeared in the model railway press criticising all manner and aspects of the micro-layout. The writers' justifications were based on the theory that trains have nowhere to run and such 'layouts' are little more than an exercise in scenic modelling. Conversely, because the standard of some of the micro-modelling has been so high, such modellers were also accused of elitism! I thus hope the content of this book raises awareness and understanding not just in this genre of railway modelling, but also in the entire hobby. So, to get started, let us first look at the benefits and advantages of micro-layouts.

BENEFITS AND ADVANTAGES

Space

- A micro-layout by its very nature occupies only a small space.
- It places fewer demands on a family home, especially in modern housing where space is at a premium.
- It's easy to store.

Handling

- It's easy to set up and move.
- Legs/trestles required to support it are kept to a minimum.
- It's self contained.
- It's easy to transport to exhibitions.
- It's accessible and easy to lift.

Cost

- It's relatively inexpensive.
- You're unlikely to get held up through lack of funds.
- It will demand low financial outlay.
- Fewer materials, stock and scenic items are required.
- If all goes wrong, or circumstances change, it's not a huge waste if it has to be scrapped.

Time

- It will take less time to build.
- You can start quickly.
- It will not demand great perseverance.
- You don't have to wait long before you see results.

Design

- You can design it to have different, interchangeable modules.
- It's easier to visualise at one go.
- It need not be 'boring' if well planned.
- It's ideal for the newcomer and especially the 'armchair' modeller.
- It's not a daunting undertaking.
- It's a blend of diorama and working layout.
- A small layout can give an intimacy that you don't get with a larger one.
- You can change your mind more easily.

Versatility

- The layout can easily be extended.
- It can be used to display static models when not being operated.
- It can be more detailed, with working accessories.
- It enables one to learn basic skills and to experiment.
- It's not likely to have troublesome baseboard joints.
- It can be easily altered to a different period or locality.

◀ Abergwynant built by Neil Rushby in 4mm scale EM, is a micro-layout very similar in principle to Bere Alston on the old L&SWR main line, though set somewhere on the Cambrian coast, rather than in Devon. Trains now run in and out of the station on their journey up the surviving remnants of the main route which is supposedly beyond the road overbridge and represented by the off-stage fiddle sidings. **See page 40 for the scheme based on Bere Alston.**

Generating Ideas

How I plan and design micro-layouts

I guess I always set myself some sort of brief about the type of layout I'm trying to design. When it's just for me, then a personal audit helps me focus on preferences; steam or diesel, industrial or rural and a time period of now or then. But of course it's not just for me. After many years of layout building my interest in the hobby has centred around inspiring others to design, plan and build layouts and therefore I cannot be quite so self indulgent. For me you have to commence with the wow factor, the visual impact. I want people to look at my designs and think… 'what a great idea,' they didn't realise it could be done so effectively in such a small space and with minimum use of resources. I want each design to be better than the previous one, which always results in an element of disappointment, as it does with any unrealistic expectation. That said, there have been some real surprises along the way and some extremely satisfying designs. These have certainly touched a chord with modellers near and far and I am grateful for the feedback from those individuals.

Successful design and planning is best broken down into achievable objectives and I almost always start by searching for an interesting railway topic. This might be something that I'm already aware of and I look for a new angle on it, or it may be something that I've just uncovered through research or a site visit.

Finding an interesting subject

There are several ways of doing this;

- Copy or develop an idea contained in this book, or other books.
- Visit real railways, operating or preserved.
- Buy or borrow suitable books.
- Surf the Net.
- Look at what other modellers have achieved in magazines, or visit exhibitions.

Take *Millfield Road* by John Wall for instance (below- see caption left for explanation).

It never ceases to amaze me where inspiration can be found. You'd expect to find it in many of the excellent micro-layouts around today, but not necessarily in a much larger layout, maybe? Well, not so, this less than a foot long section of the much, much larger *Millfield Road* by John Wall would in itself make an ideal micro. Convert it to goods only, add a single wagon traverser 6" long or so, inside the goods shed on the right and a short train traverser 18" long on the left, perhaps 'view blocked' by a girder bridge on substantial piers and masked by a backscene and an extra foreground siding.

There you have it, a micro-layout that is approximately 3' long!

Photograph: courtesy Railway Modeller.

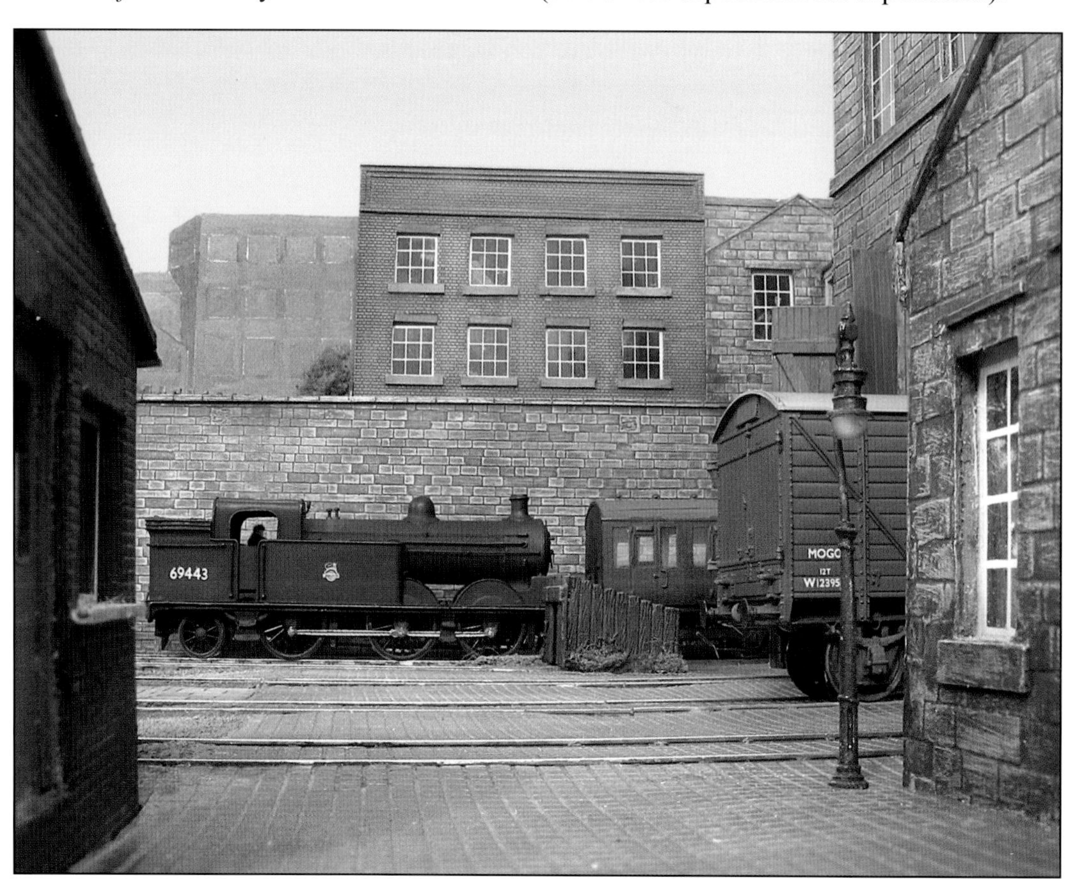

What to look for

Whatever source you use, real railways or models can vary quite dramatically from the very interesting to the not so interesting.

Here is an example of what I would call an uninteresting composition. The vertical lines of the signals, speed restriction sign, masts and platform lamps all clash with the horizontal lines of the catenery wires, tracks and train and lead the eye all over the place: there isn't really a clear focal point in the picture taken at York about 2002.

As micro-layout designers we can learn from the prototype as to what constitutes good design and what does not. This photograph taken at Edale has, in my view. many qualities of good composition; the footpath, fence and rough track all lead the eye to the focal point (signal box and train). There's a balance in shape and colour between the foreground grass and the distant hills of Kinder Scout. A Hawthorn bush left and Broom right, act as view blocks and form a scenic frame around the railway subject. A range of textures (grass, cobbles and gravel) and colours (a myriad of greens and yellows caught in the midday sun) come together to form a subtle picture. Capture these types of components in your model and you'll be well on the way to success.

By comparison
This recent photo of Whitby demonstrates an uninteresting scene with poor composition.

Here's a example of what to avoid. Whitby still has an architecturally pleasing station, but the setting has been spoiled. With little regard to heritage, an incongruous supermarket in bold red brick has blotted out a sense of balance in both shape and colour. Here, with NYMR steam trains, you have operational inspiration in a visually unstimulating setting.

Though even with this, all is not lost for this can be improved by superimposing imaginary components along with the better parts of a real scene, as indeed I have done below.

Although the juxtaposition of the old buildings of Whitby, and of course the iconic Esk bridge, is not geographically correct, the whole scene looks much more attractive and would make an excellent backdrop to a narrow layout.

All need not be lost though, my composite artwork shows how things can be improved. The station remains intact but I have removed the supermarket and replaced it with the existing heritage structures of the town. Bringing together well known Whitby landmarks; the quayside, river bridge and abbey (on the backscene), to create a pleasing composition that forms the basis of a micro-layout.

Can interesting/inspiring parts be edited together in a composite design?
Yes of course. Below a historical track plan for Whitby is shown. It scales out in 4mm/ft to a size in the order of 27' x 12' (8.24m x 3.66m) which would need to be housed in a building at least 30' long, excluding the fiddle yard! Even this relatively small prototype could not be modelled accurately, to exact scale, other than by those with extensive resources.

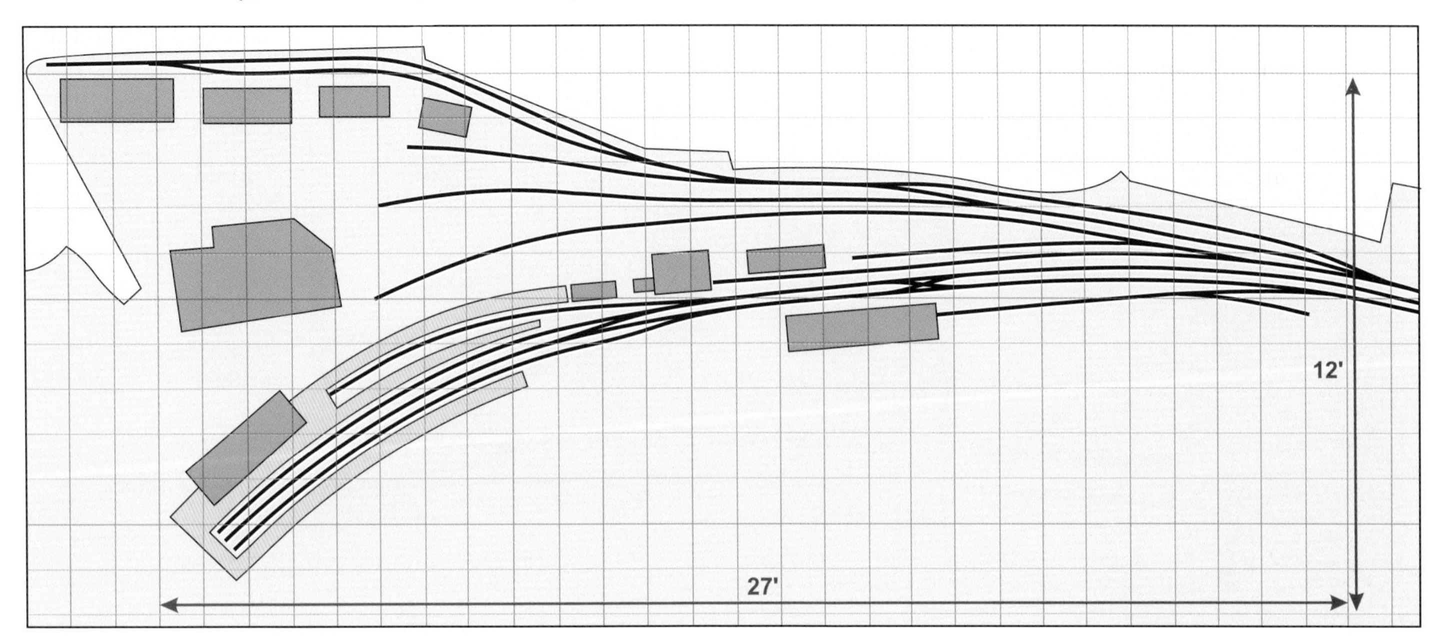

To show what I mean take a look at this 'typical' adaptation of the above prototype station, designed as a round-the-room plan. Using a relatively generous minimum curve radius of 2' 6" and allowing a platform length of 4' - 5', the overall size starts to get to about 8' x 6' - a sizeable area that would require a spare bedroom or medium size garden shed: and this plan does not have much in the way of operational potential either!

You can see however, that the plan captures many of the salient features in a fraction of the space required for a true scale model.

Composite and compromise. For years layout builders have been using track plans like this and converting them into a reduced scale size model representation that captures the salient features.

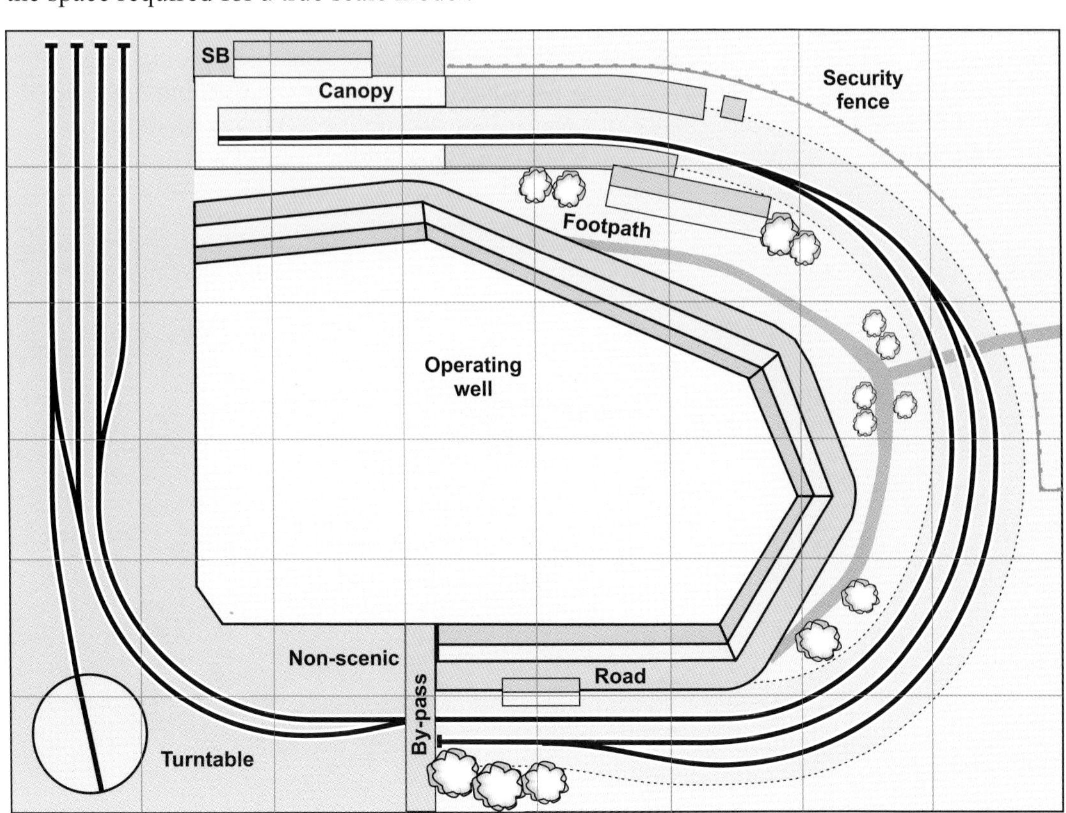

Before the advent of micro-layouts this might have been seen as a typical average size interpretation of Whitby. As you can see it is still quite large and not ideally suited to someone short of space.

Having found your ideal inspiration, can it be squeezed into a small space?
There are lots of tools and tricks that can be employed to squeeze a larger subject into a small space. These are dealt with later but for a moment consider this minimum space version of the 'typical' plan on the previous page.

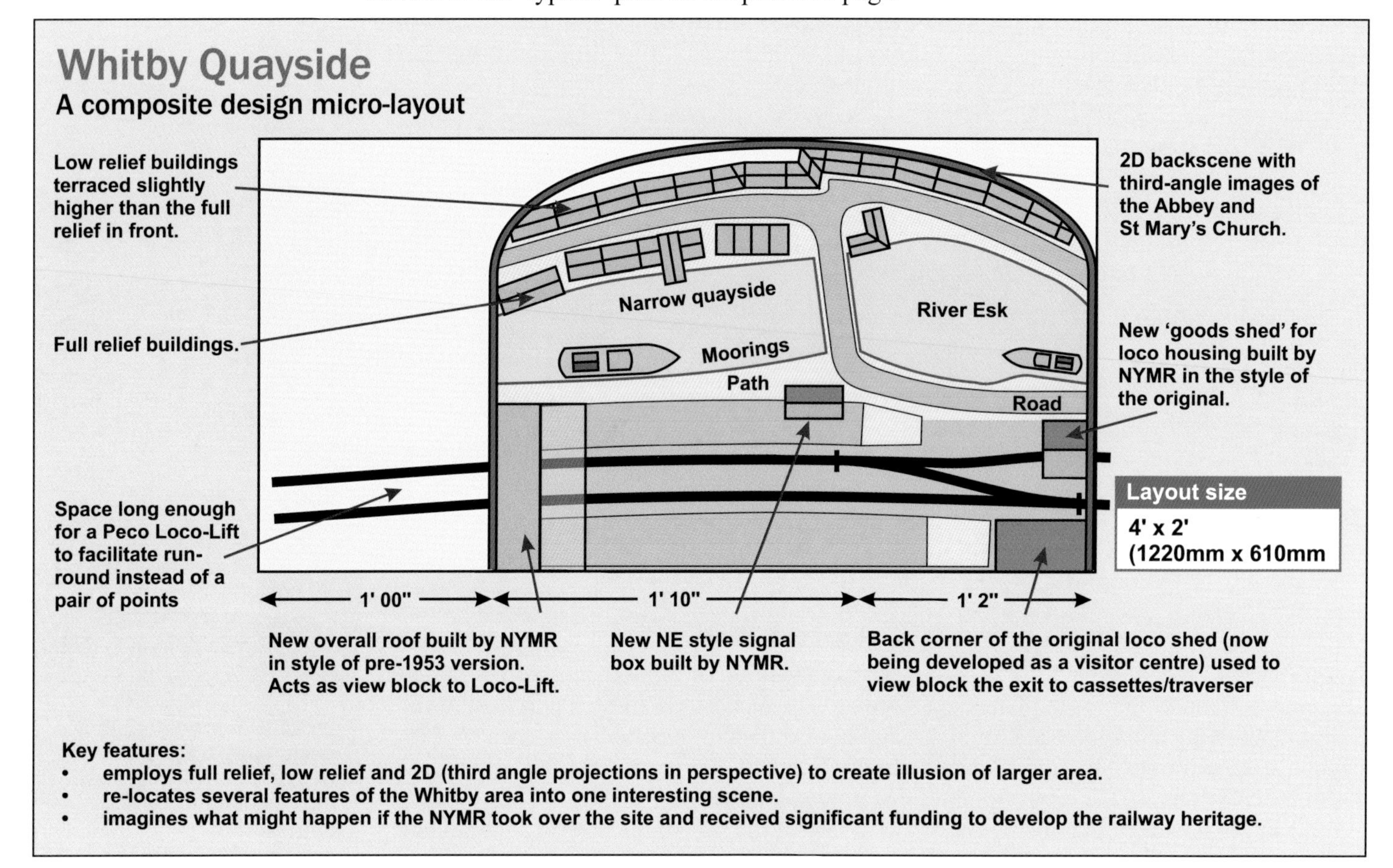

What can and cannot be incorporated?
You've got to be realistic. In a small space there has to be some major compromises. If your inspirational subject is small then the lesser the compromise. Clearly something made up of several sidings has much more chance of success than attempting to build a main line or large railway station, which are completely out of the question.

Here is a scene on David Room's 00 gauge layout *Ting Tong Yard* showing how parallel tracks, narrow grass verges, low buildings, low bodied short wheel-base wagons, all give an impression of greater length and contribute to a feel of a busy four siding layout without over-crowding

Photograph: courtesy Railway Modeller.

Tools and Tricks

Learn how to use the smallest, shortest item in a confined space whether it is a loco, a piece of track an item of scenery or a baseboard. Think minimum, absolute minimum and then any extra bit of space you can grab will be an extremely satisfying expansion.

Start with the baseboard, what shape best suits your needs? This might be influenced by the design you want to create, your chosen prototype, the location for displaying the layout, budget and so on. Your layout therefore could easily be a long and narrow shelf, a quarter circle to fit in a corner, a more traditional square or oblong for use on a table, or perhaps something a little more unusual in shape; a full circle or triangle for all round scenic viewing. The plan section later in this book has oblong, square, 'L' shaped, quarter circle, full circular and triangular layouts. Whilst there is a predominance of oblong designs, the sizes shown are quite varied. Whatever shape and size you choose, make the most of the space available.

How small can you go?

Here are some thoughts on how to get the longest run of track in the smallest possible area. I've used an oblong plan to illustrate the point but the process is the same regardless of what shape baseboard you use.

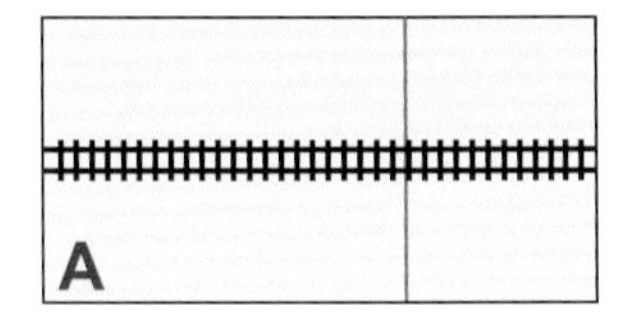

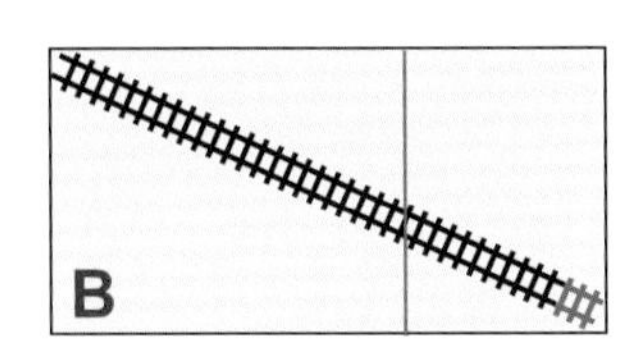

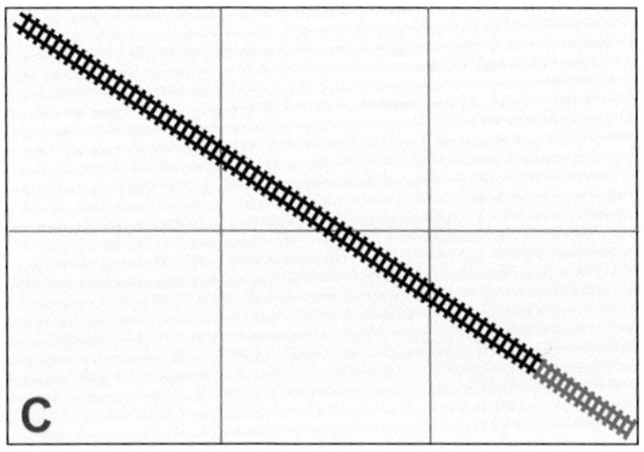

A is probably near the minimum for any kind of operation with just one loco and a couple of wagons, but has maximum use been made of the space? Certainly not, you can see the running length is 18": place the track across the diagonal as in B, and the running length increases to 19.5" OK, that's probably not an earth shattering increase, but undertake the same exercise with C. across a 3' x 2' baseboard and the increase is 6.5" that is, from 36" to 42.5", relatively substantial when you think of it in terms of a short 0-4-0 or 0-6-0 loco or an extra wagon.

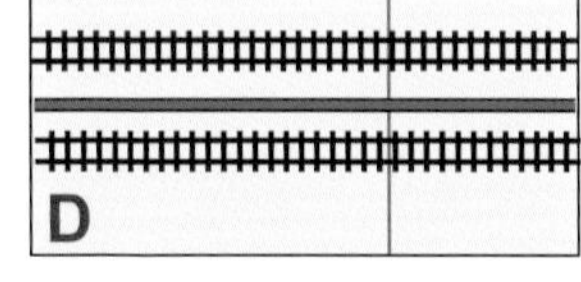

Alternatively you can further increase running length by simply dividing the board in two and having a double-sided backscene somewhere down, though not necessarily, the centre as in D. By utilising a Peco Loco-Lift to transfer between tracks, the running length on our original 18" x 9" piece of board is now 36".

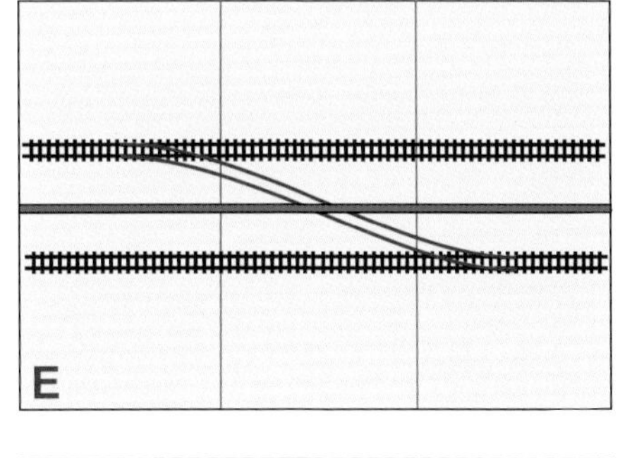

Likewise on E, our 3' x 2' board now increases to a generous 6' of running: it's also possible to fit a link between them, and if you can get any of the tracks across a diagonal, it will increase a little further.

A 3' x 2' split level layout shown at F also offers the possibility of extra operational running space, for two different trains. A combination of this and the double sided versions will get us near the absolute maximum for the size of board, though you will have to be careful not to over-crowd.

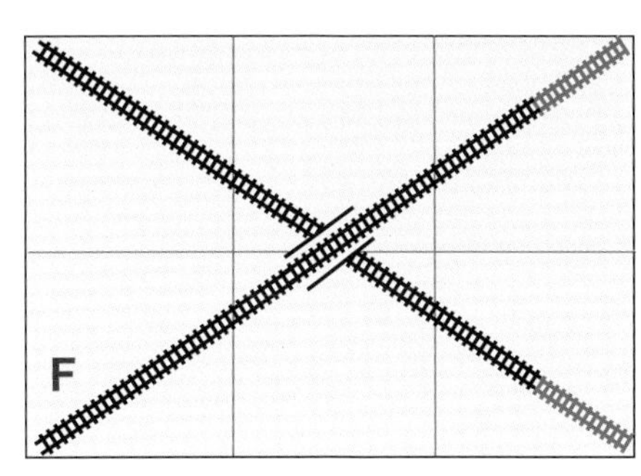

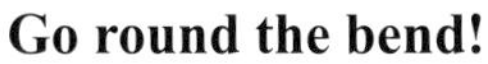

Go round the bend!

It's worth spending a moment looking at curved track especially those with excruciatingly tight radii. As with space saving across the diagonal of a baseboard, the same formula occurs when considering curved track against straight and indeed curved against diagonal. On an 18" x 9" layout (G.), track length across the diagonal is 19.5", change this to a curve and it increases to 20.5" (H). Apply this to the previous large plan C on page 13, and the increase is an additional 3.5". On test I used quite a gentle radius, if you're happy to go tighter then the running length will be increased a little further.

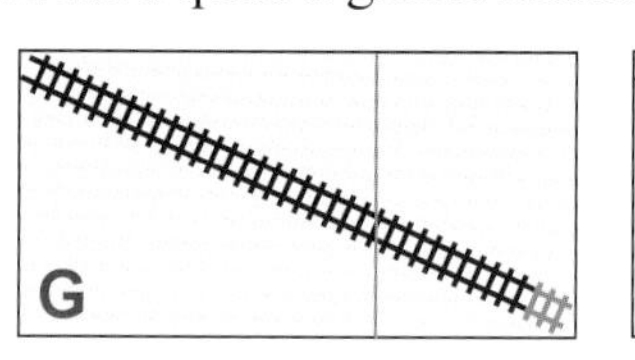

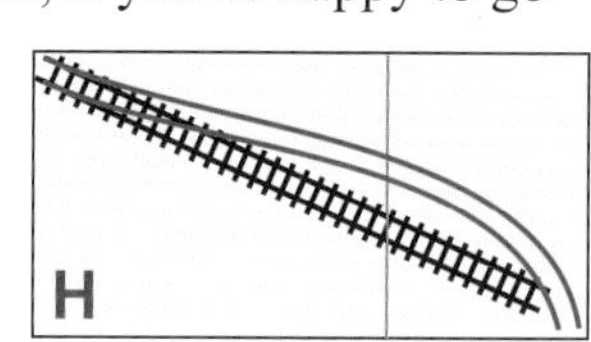

There are even tricks you can play with the track itself. By its very nature a railway line running across a baseboard will have two horizontal lines and thereby create a feeling of length. Put a second or a third track and you'll create more horizontal lines. The appearance can be further enhanced by reducing the distance between each track from the traditional 'six-foot way' to something less. You could even reduce the gap progressively more between each track as you build towards the back of a layout. This will force the perspective slightly, obviously there are some simple rules about testing the clearance on your rolling stock especially on corners where vehicle overhang becomes more pronounced. Placing tracks closer together than a manufacturer intended will have an impact on points and the like. If you're using something that fits standard geometry, like Peco Setrack, it's possible to shorten the curve so that a pair of points fit closer together. If it's not possible to reduce a point then one simple solution is to adapt the track design as shown below.

Of course, the easiest solution is demonstrated in the plan on page 36, where the layout is made up entirely of parallel tracks and has no points!

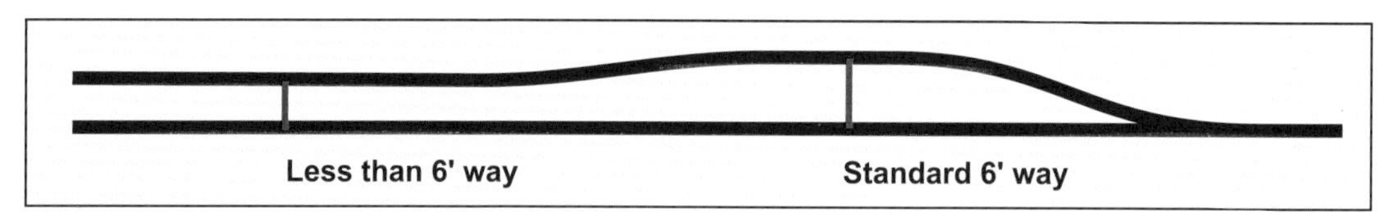

Having chosen your baseboard size, how much track can you shoehorn in: bearing my comments on over-crowding?

Take *Common Lane Wharf* for instance (below). The baseboards were approximately 4' x 2' in size and the plan incorporated many of the track features already mentioned; across the diagonal and curved sidings in particular (the front of the baseboard ran roughly parallel to the left hand side of the picture and the backscene ran diagonally as well). The run round

***Common Lane Wharf* was a ground breaking 00 gauge micro-layout built several years ago by friends Steve Best and Mike Pearson of Hull.**

Photograph: courtesy Railway Modeller.

loop was made as long as possible and was a central feature of the 'diagonal' tracks, it could just accommodate five standard vans (where three are shown in the photo). Also seen in the top left is a siding which is just long enough to take a single goods vehicle, although unlikely in prototype practice (though not entirely unknown: a short siding existed at Kielder Forest on the Border Counties route and is illustrated in *Scottish Layout Projects* by Ian Futers), it does serve the purpose of providing extra operating potential. Whilst the purists might not be impressed, it was modelled so as to look feasible and 'correct' in the context of the overall layout and is perfectly acceptable as a micro-layout design essential. So, when designing yourself, keep actual running length in mind and commence by thinking 'shortest points and crossings' with 'longest possible sidings'. Essential for achieving maximum operating potential and critical for maintaining interest!

On the topic of points, the Y point is, in most ranges, shorter than its straight counterpart: It's not just overall length that's paramount; it's the distance between the point blades and crossing V that matters, the shorter this distance the more versatile the point will be.

The Peco Streamline Y point (bottom) can easily be considered as the micro-layout builder's friend. Along with the Peco Setrack Y point (top) it has the shortest distance between frog and point blades ends; this provides the minimum distance for a split into two tracks. Although the Hornby Y point (centre) matches Peco Setrack geometry, you can clearly see the distance between frog and point blades at the toe end is greater.

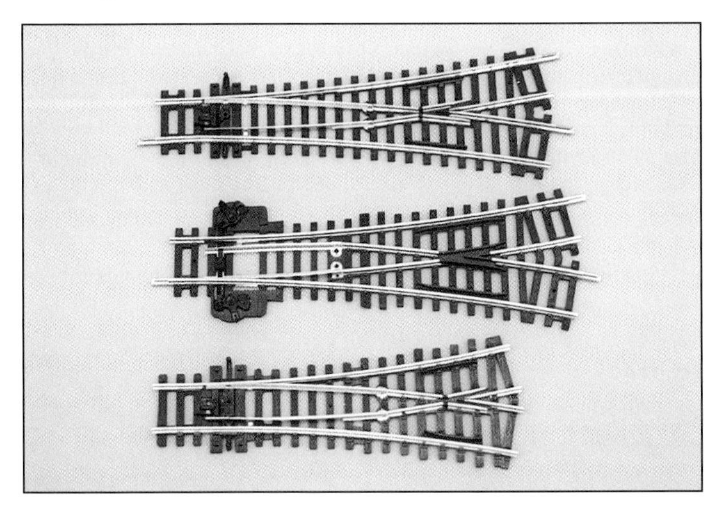

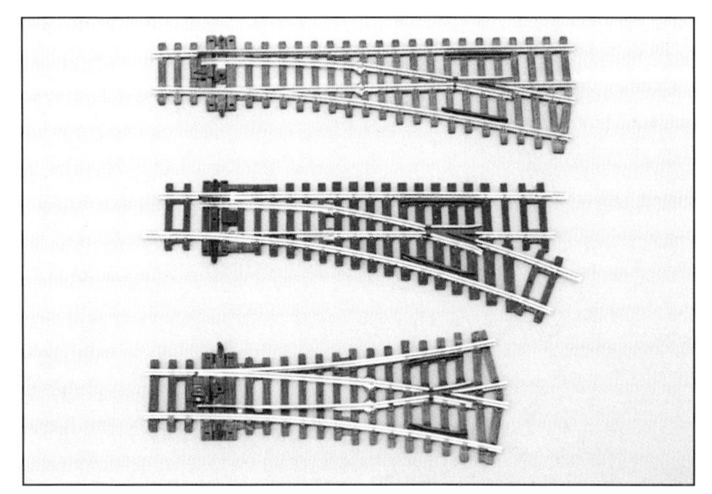

Again the gap between frog and point blade ends on the Hornby one (middle) is much less than the Peco Streamline version above it. Thus it will always be a compromise between fitting the available space and the impression you want to create. Of course, the Streamline Y (bottom) is considerably shorter than both the Hornby and Peco examples: for the micro-layout builder this means you can curve away sooner - and thus save valuable inches - than you can on the straight track of a standard point.

Three-way points can offer even greater space saving where more than two sidings are required. Even two of the incredibly short Peco Streamline Y points, giving three sidings, are longer than both their symmetrical and asymmetrical three-way points. So these particular track items can be indispensable especially so for fans of hidden sidings.

A similar, though less complicated, situation exists with diamond crossing and double slips. The double slip effectively packs in two points laid toe to toe and can be even shorter than two of the shortest Y points laid in this way.

For micro-layout applications always find ways of utilising the shortest points and crossings so as to give maximum possible length to the running lines and sidings.

The next design consideration is train length.

Prototype Micro Trains

In modern times most trains are quite long. That's certainly true of today's company trains though if you look hard enough you will always be able to find some short train inspiration on the prototype that can be transferred to your model: like this shot of a Class 47 hauling an inspection saloon for instance. Short trains are not an idea conjured up by micro-layout modellers: they've been around in the real world for years! The shortest of all of course is the light engine, a loco on its own (see Page 4: about the author), then there are those trains with one or two wagons, or the

Besides deception, my *Micro on a Plank* idea on page 38 depends on short mainline trains. Here's one that in 00 scales in at under 61cm (2') comprising of Class 47 No. 47 971 and a single inspection saloon, perfect for a scenic section of equal length.

On a diesel layout the shortest passenger train is always going to be a single railcar, be it the first generation 121/122 class, or the more modern 153 which is actually substantially longer than its earlier cousin. Having said that, 153 320, seen here at Pwllheli, still constitutes a very short train of around 305mm (1') in OO gauge. In recent times Hornby has re-released this popular model in several Privatisation liveries, so even a bang-up-to-date micro can be built.

If you're looking for a DMU for a tight space then the Hornby Class 142 takes some beating at just 405mm (1'-4") overall. Judging by the canopy shadow, the twin is not much different in length to the station buildings and as such, a station platform need be no longer than the train. Train length when planning is a given, you can't reduce them further and you need at least the same amount of distance, and probably more, for the train to travel to.

Freight trains made up of short wheel based stock are just the thing for minimum space layouts. At a pinch you'll get a short loco, either steam or diesel, and two wagons, or three wagons without a loco, or if you're very lucky, four 71mm long traditional wagons on a standard turntable or Peco Loco-Lift, which occur in several of my designs. Here in 1990, 08 054 pulls an ideal micro-train of 4-wheel stone hoppers at Swinden Quarry, near Skipton.

single railcar. To set you thinking I've included a few photographs showing some typical short trains above.

How much stock can your design handle?

The following photographs show comparative lengths of a selection of 'short' locomotives (steam and diesel) and rolling stock. All such items, being available ready-to-run (though some may be temporarily out of production) are essential motive power for the micro-layout builder.

When purchasing locos for your micro-layout don't shy away from asking your local model shop to demonstrate the space saving qualities. Get them to remove the loco's from their packaging, position them with buffers lined up at one end (as per this photo) and take a good look at overall length and overall wheelbase length. Use a rule if necessary and don't be fooled by two locos that on the surface appear to be similar in length. The blue Class 03 and green Class 06 in this photo are approximately the same length over the buffers but not over the wheelbase: the latter being somewhat shorter on the 06.

The benefit of a short wheelbase is illustrated in this shot of the Class 06 shunter. Less than one piece of Peco ST-203 (41mm long) is required for the loco to clear the Y point blades. If you look closely you can see the point blade between the right hand wheel and the curved end of the black plastic steps. Of course, it is this sort of minimum space geometry that can be used too great effect at the short end of a run-round loop.

Don't be fooled by volume either. If you ask a cross section of modellers to list the shortest locos available in 00 chances are that most would include the Terrier, right, due in part to its low height, yet this photo shows it to be equal in length to a Class 03, and its wheelbase is considerably longer!

Its easy to see why a considerable number of micro-layout builders go for traditional rolling stock with 10' and 15' chassis. With buffers lined up extreme left and right, you can compare lengths of these open and closed vehicles and check out their suitability for a particular short siding. You can use this process for all types of wagons and modern traction modellers need not be daunted by today's long, high tonnage vehicles. Fortunately there are still a number of shorter examples in use; the HAA and VDA are ideal examples.

Other Considerations

Couplings
Couplings can have a massive impact on train length. Tension lock couplings, the type used by Hornby and Bachmann, keep vehicles further apart than prototype so that they can negotiate sharp layout radii without difficulty. If the curves on your model are slight, then it's possible to resort to a space saving alternative such as the three-link coupling or some other automatic coupling. However do bear in mind that proprietary couplings are there for a purpose, so only change them if you are confident that your stock will run properly.

Visual Impact

Important as they are, don't just confine your search for minimum space to baseboard size, track and rolling stock; the same exerting demands must be placed on scenic features too. Getting the volume, balance and viewpoint right is absolutely essential. One of the most important, if not the most important aspect of micro-layout design is to create an illusion that your layout appears to be more than it actually is. We've learned how to maximise this process with track but not with scenery.

Visual perception
It would be a tragedy if an excellent track plan was wasted by ineffective scenic treatment. The main principle for success harps back to my art college days and to the time when you start to take an interest in what you wear. It's that old adage about lots of vertical lines make you look tall whereas horizontal ones make you look small. What does this mean in modelling terms? Look at the two illustrations; imagine each is a frame around a micro layout. Vertical lines, which in reality could represent tall buildings, make the overall length appear short. By contrast, a horizontal line, perhaps representing a low building, makes the overall length appear longer.

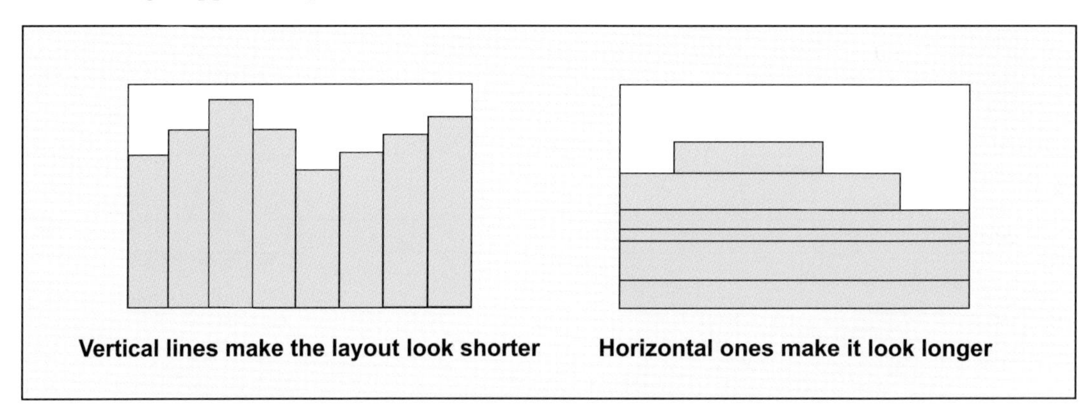

Vertical lines make the layout look shorter   Horizontal ones make it look longer

Whilst one might not want to have all low features it is important to break up high structures into narrower bands, as shown below and opposite in the photograph.

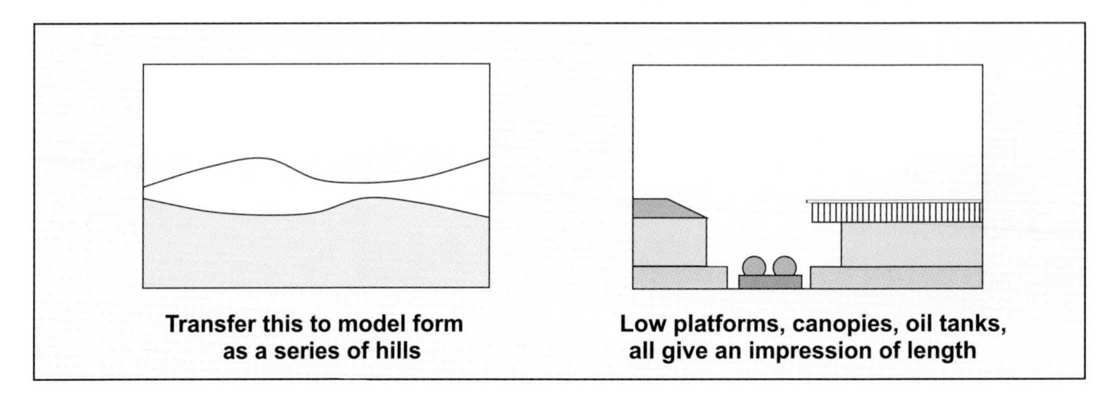

Transfer this to model form as a series of hills   Low platforms, canopies, oil tanks, all give an impression of length

There is no doubt that long low horizontal lines will give your layout an impression of extra length. It's here you can start to think of the many scenic features that exist to aid this process; pipelines, hedges and walls, lines of distant hills, parapet walls, tiered buildings, fencing and of course the track itself.

If you want to use tall buildings without making the overall layout look short it would be wise to introduce lots of horizontal lines. We can see the benefit of this process at Peak Forest. Can you spot all the horizontal components; shallow roof lines, narrow roof lights, handrail, gutters, fascia board, some pipes, girders, low stone wall, narrow roadway and the track itself.

Layout depth is important, too much will make the layout look fat and chunky, too little will render it over-crowded. You must strive for balance.

In doing that there's a lot to be learned from the prototype. One thing I've experienced over many years on my photographic surveys is that components of a railway scene are almost without exception well spread out. Yet despite this, my sweeping vision picks up all the interesting features and condenses them into what I thought I saw. You can imagine my disappointment when photographs have been printed and the reality is out of step with my imagination. I'm certain that's why I have a fascination for those extreme telephoto images that appear to move scenic features closer together - foreshortening the perspective, to call it by its technical term.

The foreshortened perspective created by a telephoto lens tends to compress distance in such a way that it appears as if the various elements in the scene are each on their own a flat layer. In essence it creates a two dimensional impression. It is the very effect that I try recreate in my designs. Because each layer appears thin, the overall length or depth of a baseboard can be squeezed up accordingly.

There's a lot to be learned here in transposing this experience to model form. By using a whole range of scenic devices from flat backscene, then half relief, then fully modelled buildings: all closely but carefully spaced you can create an image of depth in a narrow space. In fact exactly as some modellers have been doing years.

Here is an example of how to blend the foreground to the backscene. Half relief buildings have been used up against the back board itself, whilst in front of them, the models used are in full relief. Throughout the scale of 4mm has been adhered to, including the photos on the backscene which were carefully selected to match the scale as closely as possible. The layout is Ashbourne Midland by Tony Franc, David Lenton and Mark Ratcliffe.

Photographs: courtesy Railway Modeller.

Point of Exit

The process of creating realism should extend to every aspect. One weakness on many layouts both large and small, is at a point of exit where track passes from a scenic to a non-scenic section. At best this is can be disguised by an overbridge, or similar: at worst it may just be a hole in the backscene! If you have to resort to a hole, try something less conspicuous than a square or oblong aperture, I think that this aperture appears to have been neglected. Many don't mind if the fiddle yard can be seen through the hole: I think on a larger layout where there are two such breaks, it's less noticeable, as the distance between them is great, but it's not so easy on a micro as you can usually see all of the layout at once. Either way we all could do better, and although other items would work equally well, this series of mock-up photos uses trees as a device to mask a backscene aperture.

If you place view blocks, in this case three trees, in optimum position there's every chance that an exit hole in the backscene will be masked from the viewing side. Note how I have suggested in pencil how further trees should be painted or part modelled on the backscene to create a woodland vista.

Whilst it is important to keep the aperture to a minimum, its shape should reflect those items used to view block. The organic tree line has been used here to define the hole. Additionally a thin edge is preferred to thicker ply or MDF board. You can reduce the visible edge around any aperture by sanding from the back.

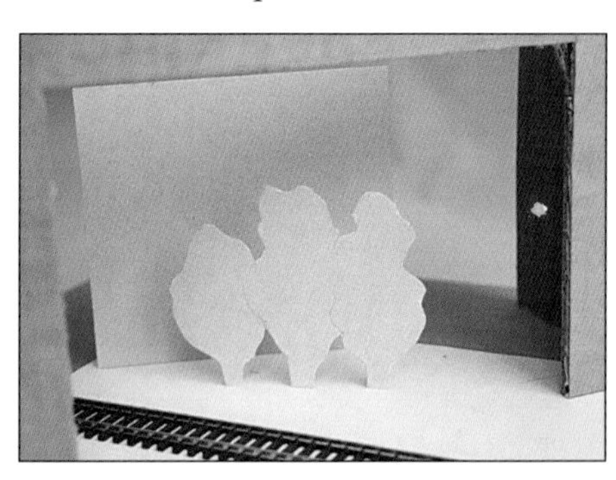

I've always been surprised that modellers by and large don't continue an element of scenic modelling onto the non-scenic section. In the shadows you can see my suggested position for further trees, which could be in 2D together with a mini backscene board blocking out any last openings in the line of vision.

Furthermore an improved result will be achieved if you can block the view behind the aperture as shown right. I accept that if your fiddle yard fits directly up to the other side of the backscene, perhaps with a traverser or fan of sidings, there may not be room for such an item as this. However on micro-layout designs, non-scenic sections are often only short lengths of single track, so such a device is probably quite suitable for micros.

The mini backscene and additional trees need not occupy a great deal of space, as seen in this view mocked-up and with the foreground detail removed.

View blockers

This brings us neatly on to the subject of view blocking generally. A view blocker prevents the viewer from seeing something that's unrealistic on the layout. Not only can a view blocker be used at the point of exit, but in many other circumstances; where 2D and 3D scenery meet, where a backscene changes direction (especially at a rear corner) etc.

Here's a section from the 3D illustration for the plan on page 32, based on St Blazey. The main exit/entry track disappears behind the water tower on the extreme left, and through a small hole in the backscene. When all viewed at baseboard level from the front, the hole in the backscene will not be seen at all. The tower therefore is a splendid example of how a 'view blocker' works to help maintain the illusion that there's more railway beyond the immediate scene.

No matter how far back you stand by *Castle Wharf Yard*, it is impossible to see any of the non-scenic section which has been successfully 'view blocked' by modeller Richard Peake who used two narrow (low relief) warehouses. When viewed at eye level from the front, the illusion of depth is really evident as seen in the inset below. *Photographs: courtesy Railway Modeller.*

Viewing angle

When all this has been achieved, viewing and staging the layout will make or break all of your hard work. To some degree the size and shape will dictate how the layout is viewed. There are however, some golden rules which tend to suggest that the narrower the layout the nearer it needs to be to eye level viewing position whereas a wider layout can be viewed from a slightly higher level. It's important to restrict the viewer into seeing only what you want them to see or any illusion you've created will be lost. Ensure that outer screening allows only the layout to be seen and that once you've focussed the viewers attention onto it make sure all the tricks you've learned; track positioning, view blocks, sound, light and so on keeps their interest firmly fixed. Avoid weak links in the process; a hole in a backscene that allows visibility into a non-scenic area will almost certainly spoil a great layout.

With many layouts, control of the viewing angle is important such that the viewer sees the layout much as the builder intended. This small 009 narrow gauge layout built by Paul Windle shows the sort of display arrangement that works best for micro-layouts.

Lighting

Good lighting is essential for effective staging. For a micro-layout, three types of lighting are best considered; that off the model which works overall or creates a mood and that on a model, like street lighting. Overall you will require a soft natural light and this can be achieved by using neon tubes. Take great care to position your lights so as not to cast unnatural shadows across the backscene, scenic flats and buildings in full and part relief. Note that the closer these are to each other the more difficult the task will become.
Mood lighting is almost certainly going to come from one point, although there are exceptions. In the case of the former a soft red spotlight can be used to suggest a sunset or sunrise, a brighter, white spotlight to suggest the sun and to cast appropriate shadows, a dimmer switch on the spotlighting will facilitate different degrees of daytime light.

Of course, it's possible to dispense with overall lighting and settle for using just the lights on the model itself: street or yard lamps, interior lights and so on. Though it's probably wise to have overall lighting as a standby.

Right: lights, such as spotlights that cast strong shadows on the backscene are best avoided (note that these shadows were caused by photographic lamps and not layout lamps): use a neon tube instead.
Far right: model lighting can be used to create mood, as Jack Burnard's Gauge 1 micro-layout *North Hetton Colliery*, so ably demonstrates.
Photographs:courtesy Railway Modeller.

A carefully placed mirror can make a small layout look considerably large as here on Aberalyn, an N gauge layout from Gareth and Daniel Jones.

Photograph: courtesy Railway Modeller.

Mirrors

Used wisely, mirrors are a great way of making an area look larger than it is. It's a method interior designers have used for years. The reflection appears as a continuation of reality and it's in perspective. You can use a mirror as an end backscene used full height and width, or a smaller mirror can be framed with buildings and an overbridge to suggest the tracks continue through the gap and onwards elsewhere.

Forced perspective

This is another way of enhancing the available space. As we're modelling on a narrow board, even in 00 gauge, structures to the rear of a layout appear large and as visually dominant as those close to the front. By modelling these rear structures at a smaller scale the visual distance will appear greater. A gradual reduction in scale from OO through HO, TT to N works better, though not always, than a sudden change from say, OO to N.

A subtle bit of perspective modelling has been created in this OO gauge village scene by Ken Harland. Note how the buildings gradually change from full to half relief then are completely flat. The distant ones are yet to be painted.

Photograph: courtesy Railway Modeller.

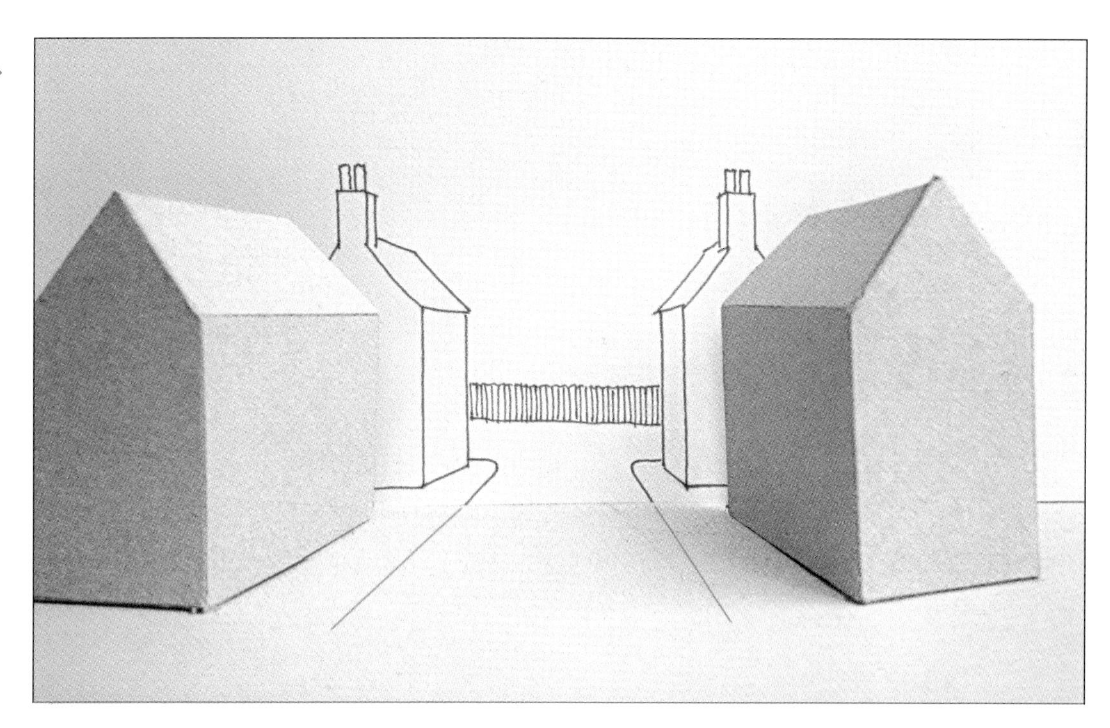

Any device that helps your micro layout look larger is well worth consideration. Modelling buildings in forced perspective takes time and perseverance and you have to severely restrict the viewpoint to eye level. In this mock up the 3D models taper towards the backscene. The foreground roadway rises up to the rear and in the direction of the horizon line, it's not flat on the baseboard surface, which is a common mistake and easy to make. Also the building lines of the 3D models must be in line with those on the 2D drawing otherwise the perspective fails.

Here we have a different method of forced perspective in that the church and distant trees are modelled to a scale of about 1mm/ft, whilst the foreground fence, bush tracks and train are all to 4mm/ft. The total width of the scene here is about 250mm (10"). This works well again at eye level, and as the church is modelled in full 3D the illusion of distance is preserved along the length of the layout. Move the eye upward however and the illusion fails. Controlling the viewing angle is therefore quite critical if we are to fool the eye effectively.

Photograph: courtesy Railway Modeller.

Sound effects

The benefit of sound on all model railways is gradually coming to prominence with the increasing availability of DCC sound-chipped proprietary locomotives. On a micro-layout it is especially beneficial, both for the purpose of adding an extra dimension to the model and in creating an illusion of more space. In the case of the latter, a distant sound effect; a passing express train, the clang of buffers from wagons being shunted and a steam loco whistle are just a few ideas that might mislead the viewer into thinking there's more to the layout than there actually is. Such distant sound effects might be produced digitally on a PC and played back via a CD player and speaker beneath the layout. In the case of the former - the DCC sound equipped loco - adding more direct up-front interest: there is now available off the shelf a substantial range of locomotive sound effects ideal for the minimum movement circumstances of a micro-layout; or simply just for the 'just ticking-over' noise whilst the loco pauses between turns. The arrival of digital sound brings an all important extra dimension to railway modelling that is far more suited - in my opinion - to the micro-layout setting, rather than getting lost amongst the ambient cacophonous noise that always seems an intrusive and unrealistic feature of larger layouts in exhibition halls.

Planning for real

Creating and verifying your plan

Now you have a few tricks up your sleeve: get planning your layout. Oh yes, before you start, I'm often reminded by modellers and editors alike of a golden rule: a train, however short, occupies a given space; and it needs the same amount of space to have journeyed from as the amount of space it is to journey to. This space is, as an absolute minimum, about three times the length of the train being modelled, though it could actually be as short as just twice the length of the train. Like all rules there are exceptions which I have explained, where relevant, in the themes and schemes section.

Now with that little 'rule' out of the way, get started with a few doodles, but if you are short on inspiration, look at the plans section to help get started. Once you're happy with your basic design, transfer it into a scale interpretation. There are templates, stencils and various types of computer software to aid this process, but my tried and tested way of using paper templates and/or track parts themselves shuffled around on a piece of paper at full size is particularly enjoyable and, indeed, an accessible method for everyone.

This only solves part of the design process by giving a 2D footprint of what will happen at ground level. It does not show how structures will appear and what volume they will occupy in 3D. It's this crucial part that will render a layout visually pleasing or not. Poor scenic planning will ruin the best track plan.

Many rudimentary items found around the home can be used for planning and designing in 3D. It's a great way of getting the feel of a layout, especially visual balance, ensuring for example all the scenic volume does not end up at one end of the layout.

Of course this is really a quick-fix solution and costs very little in time and money. Alternatively you might wish to check by building a scale mock-up. In this way you can be very accurate not only about the appearance of the track plan but also of structures and vegetation. I think, these days, all too many modellers settle for ready-made buildings and trees etc., and whilst quite excellent, often they have the wrong proportions. We should consider this issue more so in railway modelling at any size, but it's particularly noticeable with micro-layouts.

Although there are several software packages around these days to help with planning, for me there's nothing quite as satisfying and inexpensive as this method. Full size points and the paper point templates that are available from Peco, plus a roll of lining paper at £2 or £3 from most of the DIY stores is all that is required for hours of endless micro activity. Added to this view is a grouping of household packaging representing the left hand end of the plan on page 32.

Over the next few pages are several quarter scale mock-ups from card cereal packets, corrugated card boxes and Hornby plastic track templates to represent the actual track plan. They are illustrated together with full colour scale plans. The idea here is that there is a display case, into which any of the four micro-layout designs will fit. Effectively, we have four layouts in the space of just one. Although I have shown some of my favourite locations, which I often return to, like British Oak, they all are suitable for adaptation to your preferred geographical location or historical period. If like me you're easily bored with one layout, the thought of having four is an absolute delight, one of the great benefits of micro-layouts. These quarter scale mock-ups together with the relevant 2D drawing are the product of looking at what can be achieved in the absolute minimum space of 72cm square (2'-4" square). I have attempted to show that even at such a restricted space, all the layouts are quite different and each has considerable operating potential. You will note that all the designs make use of track positioned across the diagonal, for greater running length within the given space, and all have the same baseboard shape to fit the universal display case.

And the point of planning for real? You can check and change, does it fit, does it look right, and is it what you want? Keep changing and re-arranging until you're satisfied. When you are completely satisfied, that's the time to start building.

Module 1: a Branch Station

This branch station similar, though simpler in design to the plan on page 42 (Retro Railcar), can operate a single railcar or short coach and loco passenger service, together with shunting in the siding and platform line. There is a modest non-scenic section served by a sector plate. Here the longest siding will hold a railcar and the shortest a loco.

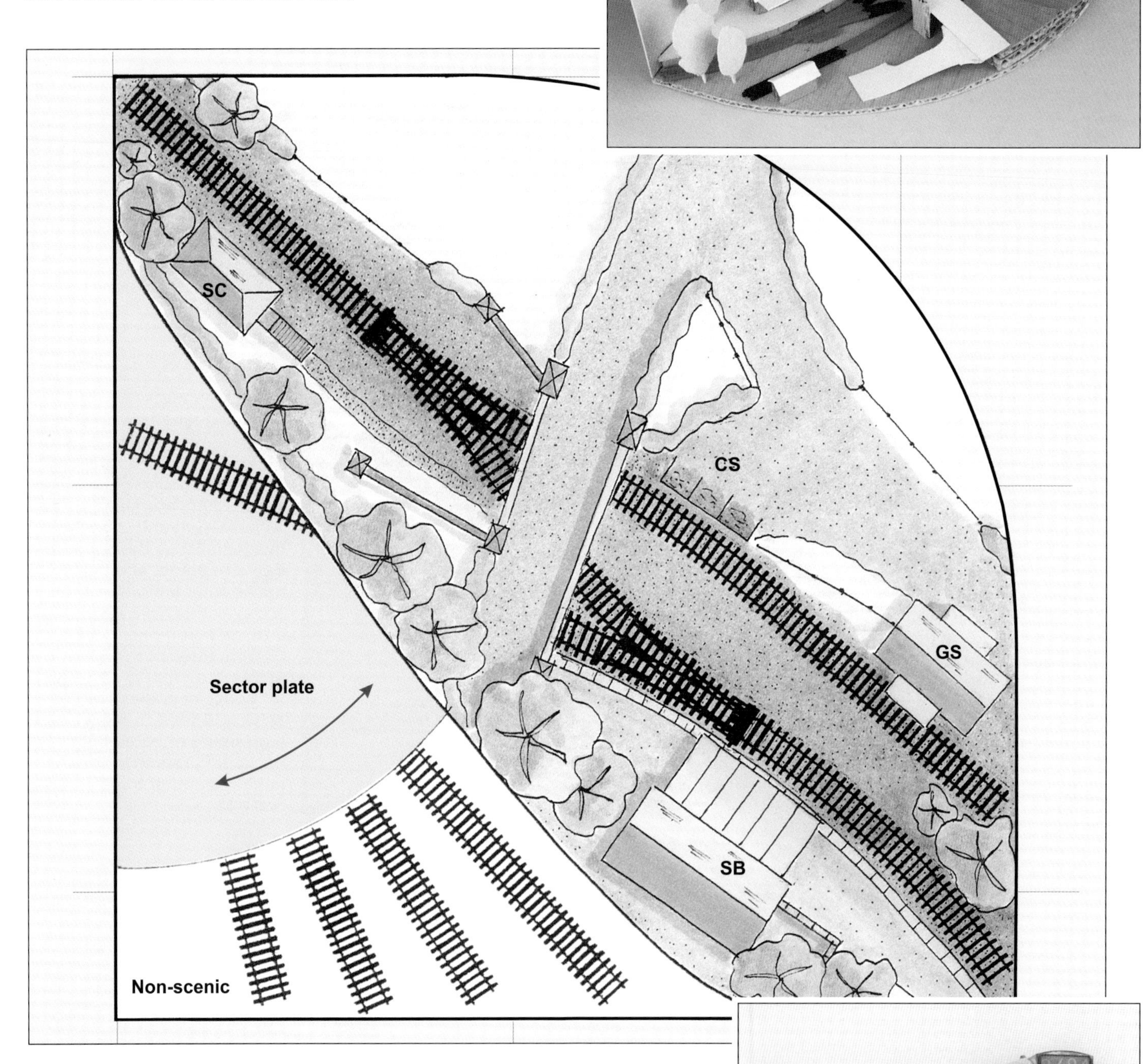

Layout size

**2' 4" x 2' 4"
(712mm x 712mm)**

Gunnislake in 1975. The station had a wonderful micro-layout sized station building. Try to imagine the first vehicle of set 480 as a single railcar and you have the inspiration for this design.

Module 2: a Wagon Workshop

Based on Radstock Wagon Works, the design makes use of short wheelbase wagons of the types; PCA, PCV, and a couple of shunters. Wagons can be moved to and from various lines and a Peco Loco-Lift inside the works will allow for stock to be changed off-stage. For those wanting a larger loco, albeit static, the layout has a display line. If you want to be faithful to the prototype, a Class 31 or 35 would be accurate.

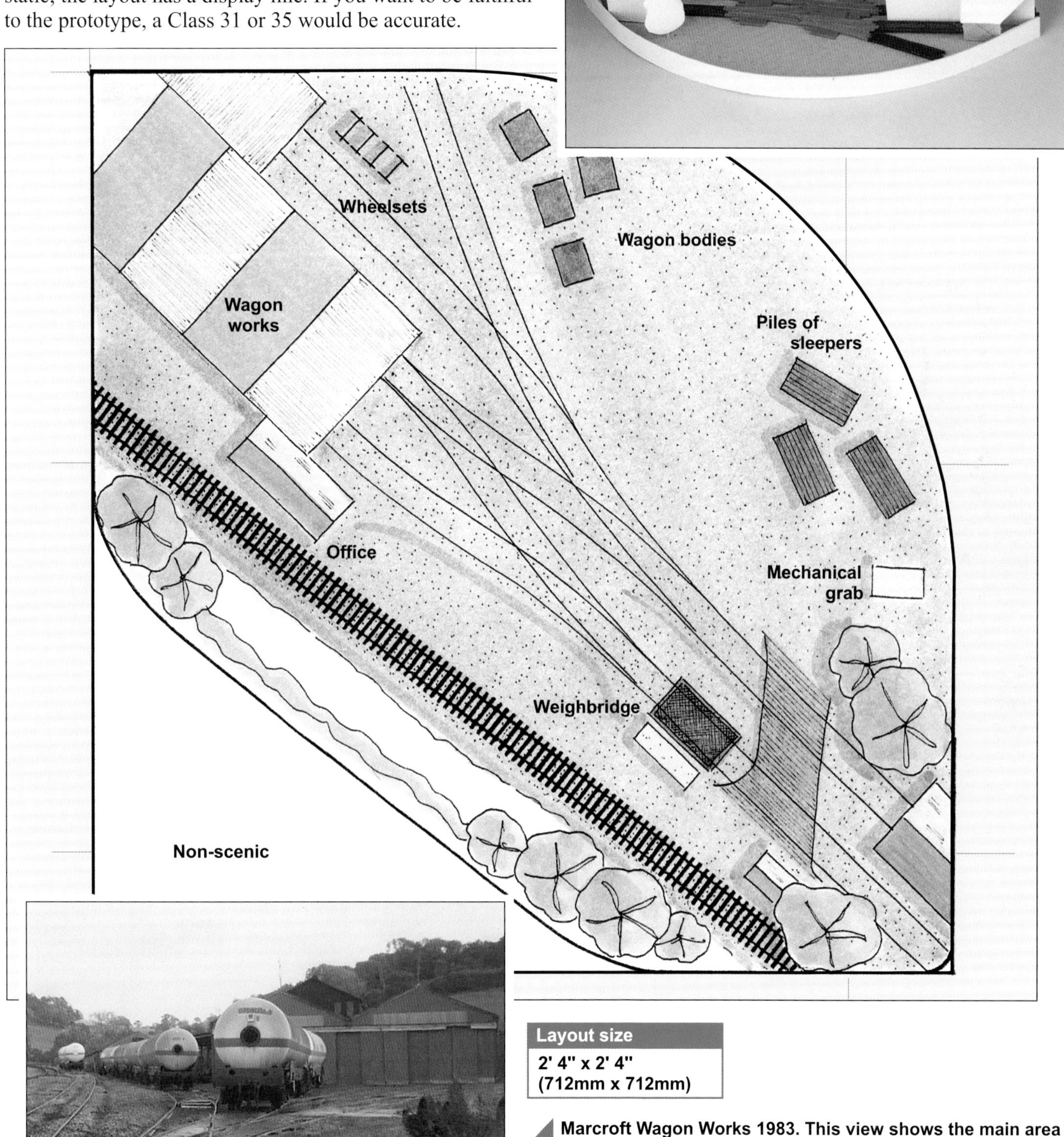

Layout size

2' 4" x 2' 4" (712mm x 712mm)

Marcroft Wagon Works 1983. This view shows the main area of the wagon works micro. The front of the model is to the right and the embankment forms the rear, against the backscene. Don't be put off by the long wheelbase tankers in this un-typical shot devoid of anything shorter.

Module 3: Milford Haven Docks

The Haken side of Milford Haven docks has always struck me as a prototype suitable for a micro-layout. I have prepared several plans set at this location over the years, including one for sectional track. On this plan there are three sidings for shunting; canopy, goods shed and crane line, and two kick-back sidings into the loco shed which was situated under the road bridge, used here as a scenic break.

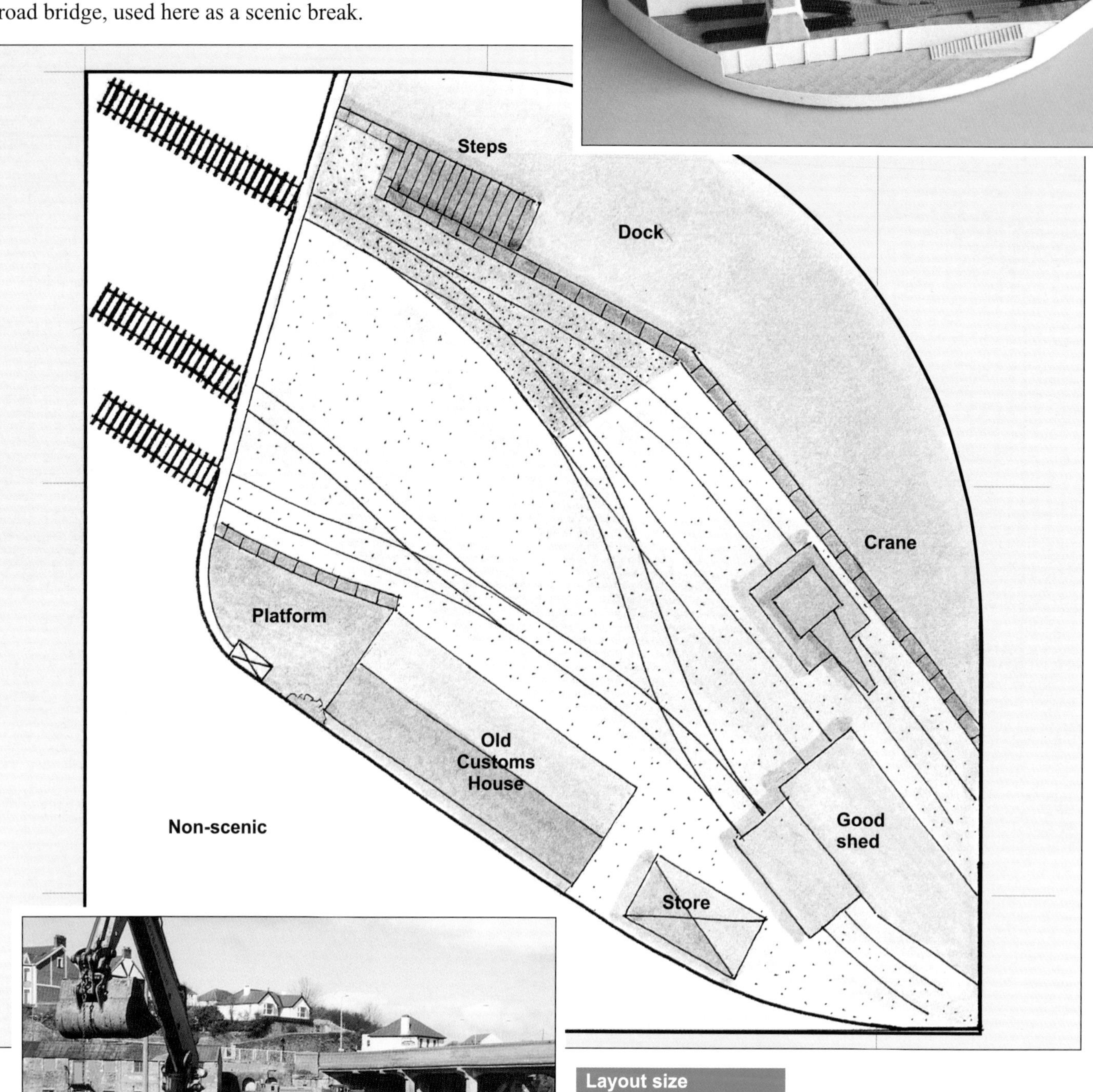

Layout size

2' 4" x 2' 4" (712mm x 712mm)

Approximately half of the inspiration for the mock-up can be seen in this across-the-water shot of Milford Haven. I have incorporated most of the features including the entrance to the under road bridge loco shed.

Module 4: British Oak

British Oak Coal Disposal Point is one of my favourites. Besides the obvious coal traffic it was a maintenance depot for industrial locos from around the north of England and saw a variety of them on test and repair. There are two sidings to shunt and two distinct places for loco movement. In addition, I have provided a set of three storage roads of approximately equal length and these are accessed via a sector plate. Here's another example of why mock-ups are essential: compare the plan and model and note how the backscene and embankment will need re-working if sufficient space is to be provided for the non-scenic section.

This view is taken a little beyond the hoppers marked A on the plan. You can see the rear of the loco shed with lean-to and the hoppers, shaped to fit the site, which have solid side walls on the model to hide the sector plate. Extreme right is the hedge which masks the stream when viewed from this side.

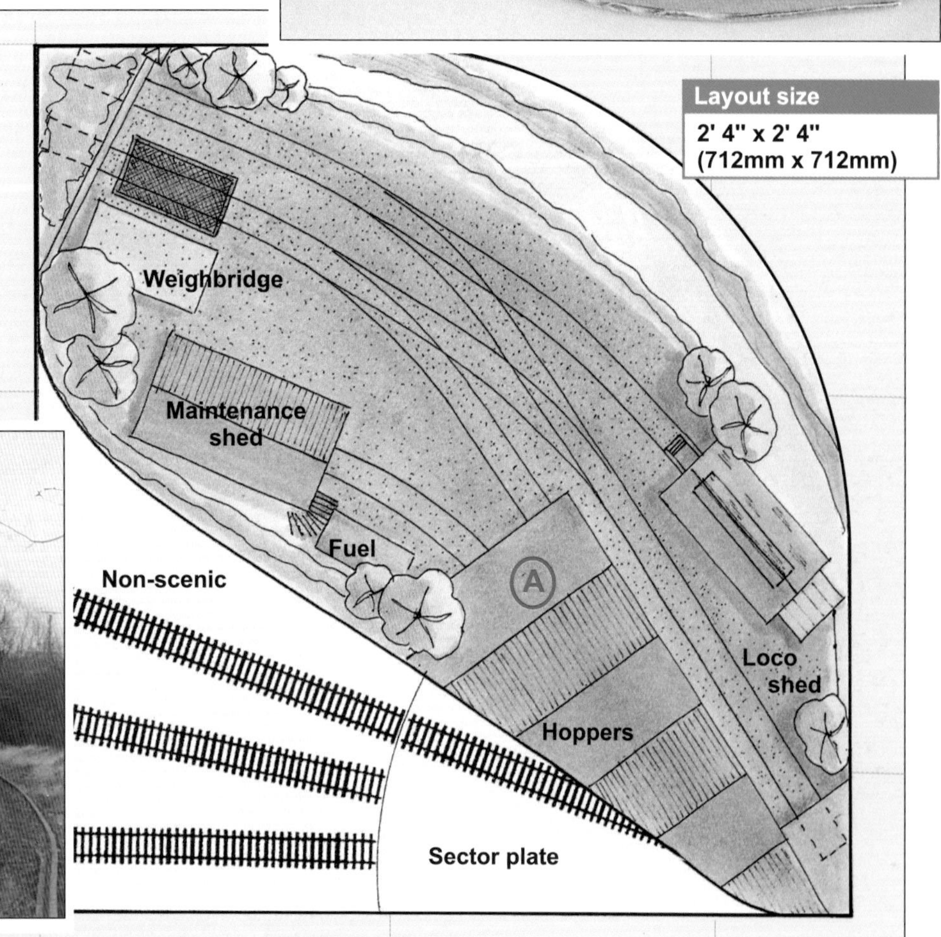

This is a mock up of the main display unit which may contain integral lighting. The idea is that any one of the four modules can be slotted into the unit for operating sessions.

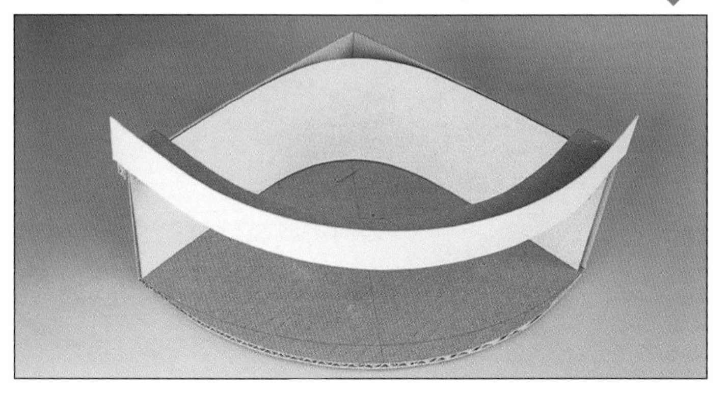

This side-on view gives a good idea of what the model of British Oak might look like when displayed. It is also useful for highlighting errors, like the tree that is too tall.

Micro-gallery

Selected examples of the genre

Before we venture into the plans section, here is but a handful of some of the micro-layouts that have appeared over the last few years: each one inspiring in a way that successfully whisks you off to the time and place portrayed. That, to my mind, is what railway modelling is all about: and if it can be done micro-size then that's got to be all the better.

Left: another view of the East Anglian freight only byway, *Saxlingham* by Dave Tailby.

Right: an overview of the 6' long scenic section on David Roome's Ting Tong Yard: only 1' wide down its length and incorporating many of the visual tricks outlined previously.

Far right: Steve Mitchell's Aston Yard. At around 4' long it too was built using many of the space saving devices found in micro-layout design.

Top right: an overall view of the award winning *Common Lane Wharf,* created by Steve Best and Mike Pearson.

Main picture: at 6' for the scenic section, Dave Tailby's *Jubilee Sidings* is probably regarded as a bit too large for the micro-layout tag, however he too used all the scenic tricks and techniques outlined in the main text and created a versatile multi-locality layout.

St Blazey

The absolute minimum

There's no 'train' shorter than a light engine (a loco on its own) and the minimum distance for realistic operation has to be a little bit more than twice its own length from scenic to non-scenic section. Take this theory, apply it to a loco roundhouse and you have the workings of an absolute minimum space railway. Clearly the locos don't go off shed, they get changed within it. It's all an illusion that will appear credible to an onlooker if the uses of stock and tracks are varied and if a loco being turned diverts concentration.

St. Blazey in Cornwall forms the inspiration here, and although no longer connected to the rail network the main building enjoys listed status and is protected for future generations to enjoy. Modellers would do well to visit the Engine Shed Society website for further information.

Operation centres around locos being turned and dispatched to one of the five stables or the water or coal line. Access depends on the length of loco used and a Peco Loco-Lift is essential for removing or adding stock on the non-scenic section.

Although my sketch shows seven radiating arms, the scale track plan, devoid of points, consists of only six and will be easy to lay with only the turntable installation providing any complexity. Scenically, many ready

Layout size

2' 2" x 1' 10"
(660mm x 550mm)

At a glance

- **Interesting operation in a minimum space of four square feet.**
- **Operate as though locos were going on and off shed.**
- **Extra track length gained by positioning across the diagonal.**
- **Layout could be themed to suit own taste, see next plan for further prototypes.**
- **Add digital sound and lighting to create more atmosphere.**

made or kit built structures could be employed though the unusual shaped shed roof will require scratch building if the style of the original is to be recreated. Similarly, vacuum tanks custom made from tubing and placed either side of the turntable would be appropriate. A photo in a back issue of British Railway Modelling (see right) shows the vacuum tanks in considerable detail.

Want to know more?

- **Engine Shed Society** abrail.co.uk/ess.htm
- **St. Blazey, British Railway Modelling, Vol 1, No 4, July 1993, page 26 and 27, includes a history and description together with two very useful photographs and a track plan.**
- **There have been open days at St. Blazey in the past and intending modellers may wish to check the EWS website.**
- www.trainspots.co.uk **includes information on the site together with wide range of pictures taken in the diesel era.**

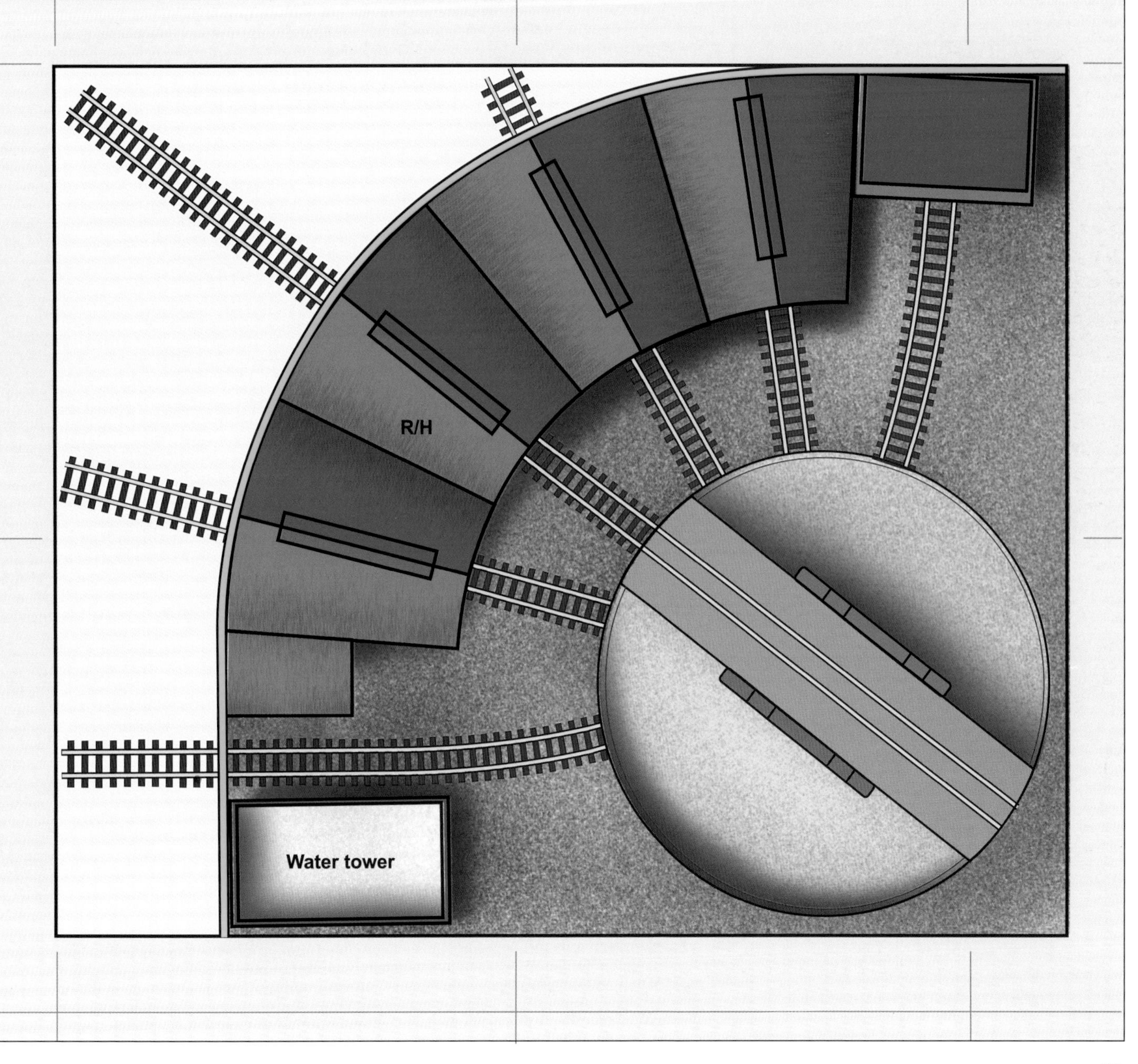

Barrow Hill Depot

The case for a Micro!

Unlike St. Blazey on the previous page, Barrow Hill has its radiating tracks and turntable contained entirely within the principal building. As such it's possible to model the site as if contained in a box with viewing by the operator/spectator from one open side. The opening side can be hinged and when moved through 180° forms a title board to the layout. The lid of the box contains non-scenic storage roads on the inside so when opened, one of these lines up with track on the scenic section; the others, which are parallel to it, are accessed via a Peco Loco-Lift. Lid depth should be sufficient to allow for a removable padded base to protect the track and the remaining depth is used as a stock storage box.

As a preserved railway, open access at Barrow Hill makes it ideal to research. A visit with camera and notepad will almost certainly result in enough information being acquired to build a realistic model. Those of you wanting something slightly more varied, if somewhat clinical, might consider the main hall of the National Railway Museum.

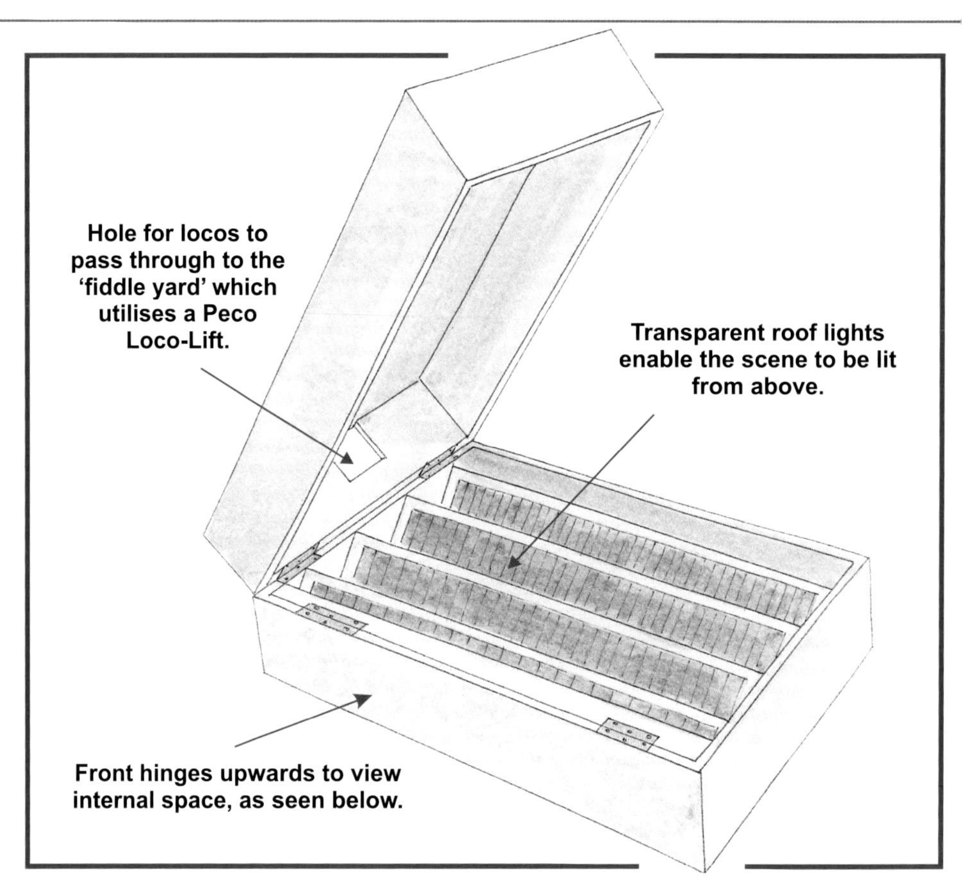

At a glance

- **A self contained portable layout and stock box.**
- **Opens up into display unit which could be taken to an exhibition.**
- **Includes combined fiddle yard.**
- **See also comments for St Blazey.**

Want to know more?

- **Barrow Hill Society-** bhess.shu.ac.uk/
- **National Railway Museum-** nrm.co.uk

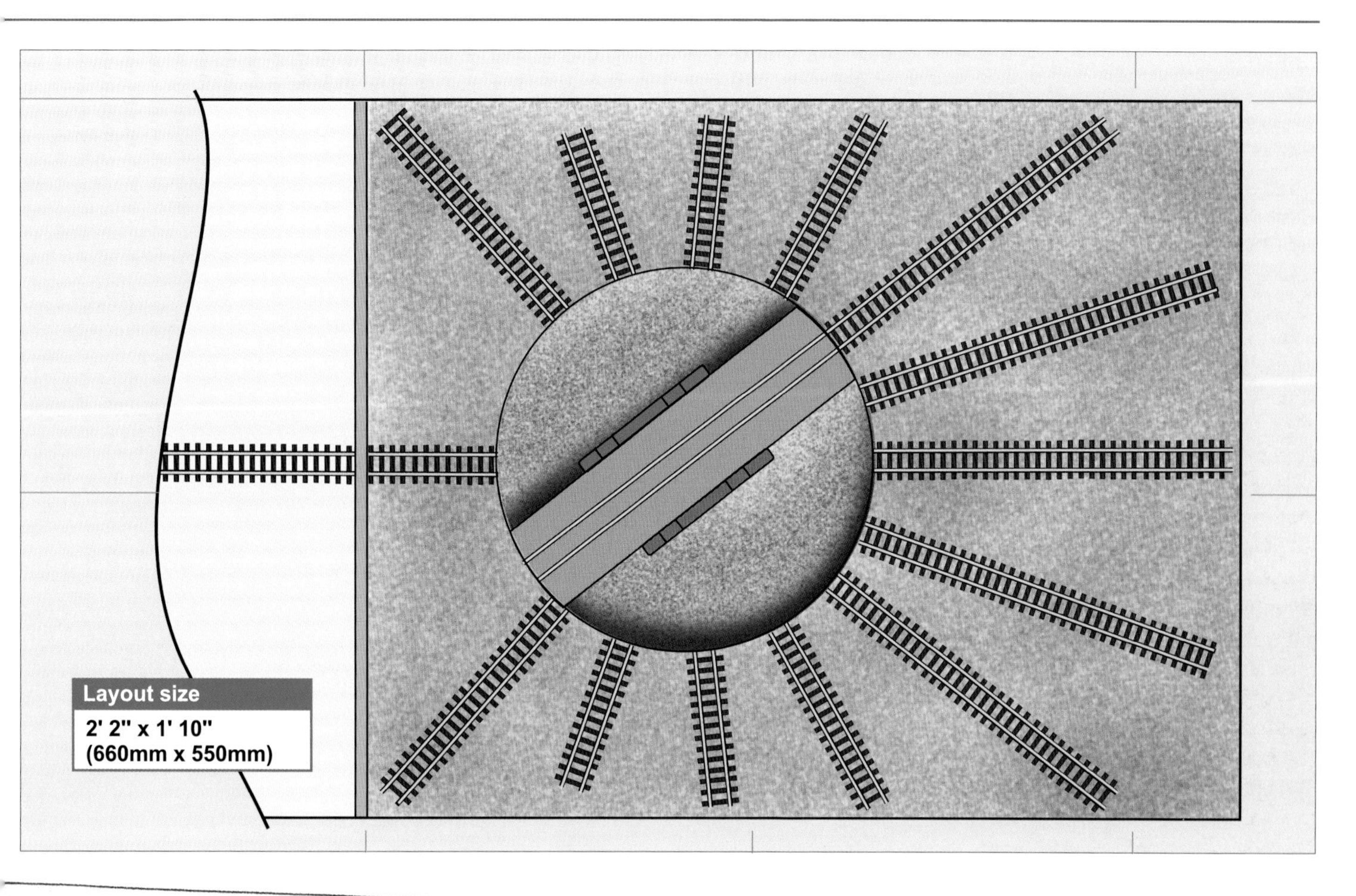
Layout size
2' 2" x 1' 10"
(660mm x 550mm)

Scenic Storage

With no points!

A micro-layout designer should always be on the lookout for any device that saves space. Clearly, one that combines fiddle yard and scenic section meets the criterion.
Here we have two identical sized baseboards, one of which slides like a traverser to allow trains to move between tracks.

Trains can be marshalled on one side of the layout by using the other side to access any line. The train is now ready to depart to the opposite end of the layout where it can again be re-marshalled, perhaps with other wagons, for the return journey.

Although designed mainly for freight wagons, a two car DMU could just be accommodated within length of each siding: it would of course have to be on a Branch Line Special.

At 4' x 2' the micro-layout is entirely self contained, but don't forget a Peco Loco-Lift could be used on open ended sidings.

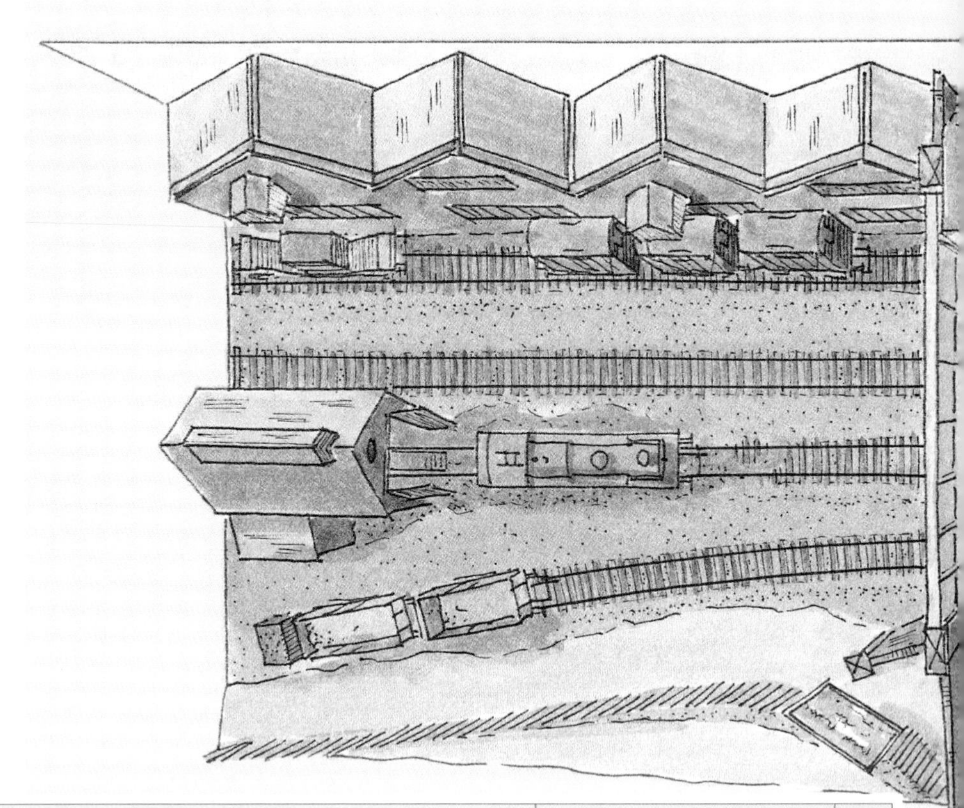

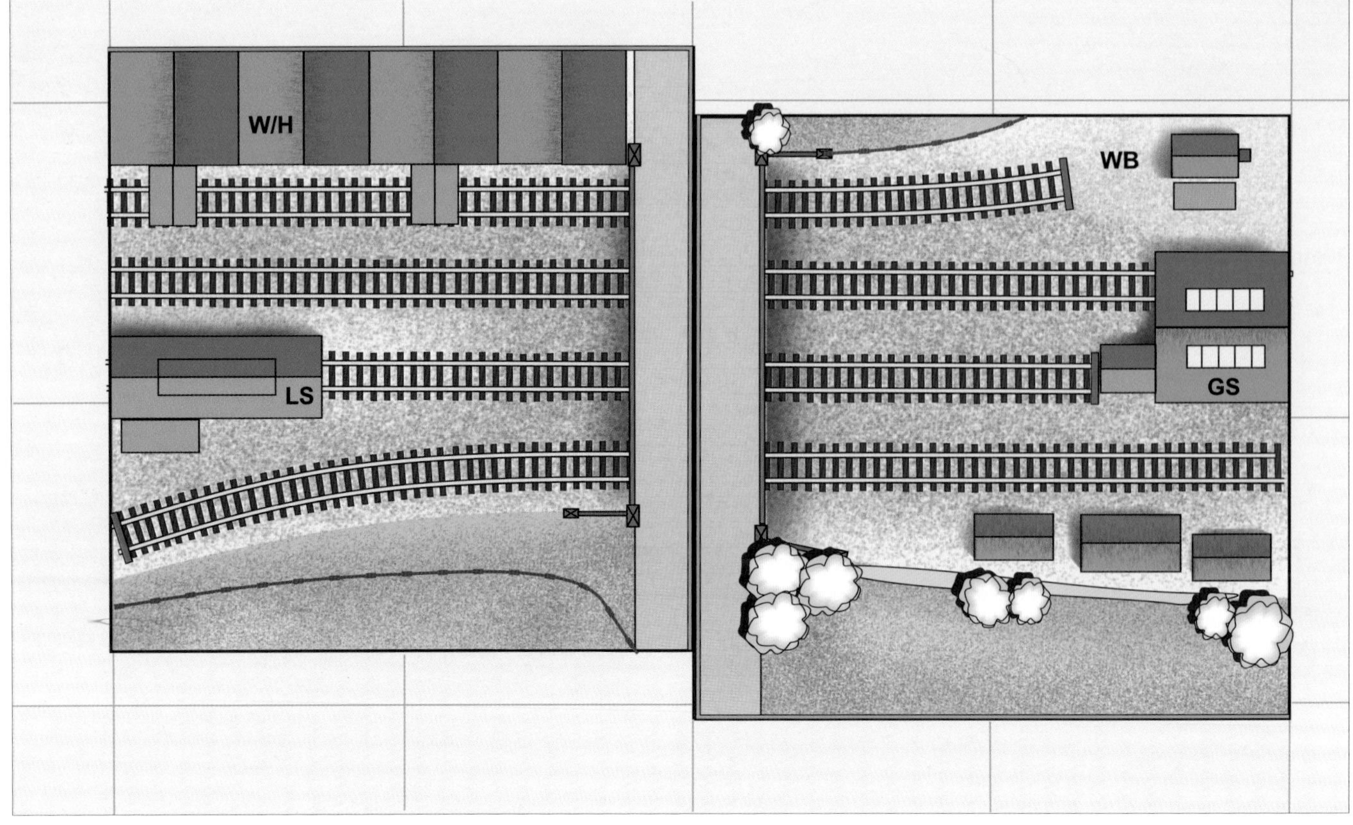

At a glance

- One side acts as a traverser.
- Both sides of the layout are used as scenically-treated fiddle yards.
- Low cost track design with no points and no possibility of locos stalling over insulated frogs.
- No tight radius curves, will allow for the use of scale, and therefore, more closer coupling.
- All tracks share common spacing where the traverser meets the fixed board.
- Layout can be run as two yards with trains dispatched one to the other.

Want to know more?

- Next Steps in Railway Modelling, Ellis C., Midland Publishing, ISBN 1 85780 171 7, Ch. 3, pages 14 to 24. The section deals with all aspects of coupling and uncoupling.

Layout size

4' x 2'
(1220mm x 610mm)

This 1991 view of Haverfordwest yard with its parallel tracks and variety of storage sheds is key to at least one half of this design; all you have to do is imagine a road bridge roughly in place of the footbridge (that I was standing on whilst I took the photograph) across the tracks.

Micro-Main Line

Inspired by Penrith and Berwick upon Tweed stations

This is one of the longest layouts in the book and on first consideration may be seen as outside the size of a micro-layout, it's certainly greater than 4', recently proclaimed in the model railway press, by some, as a cut off point. I guess my take on this is that a 4' x 2' layout equates to 8 sq. ft. whereas this one, at 6' x 1', is only 6 sq. ft. or so, so which is greatest? I'll leave that one for debate!

It's almost impossible to imagine a through main line station as a micro-layout given the accepted train length. So it's clear that any such attempt would have to use some form of deception on reality. With the end boards (which could be made as traversers) added and opened out this layout can handle a through train 61cm (2') in length; not the sort of dimension associated with a main line express! The solution is to show only the locomotive and one coach (see illustration). The train arrives at the station showing part of one coach, implying there are more coaches off stage, the locomotive uncouples and runs round using the rear line (either transferred by hand, loco-lift or traverser if built that way). The train then draws out from whence it came, as often happened on the prototype, without it being obvious there's only one coach. The layout is of course capable of handling a two car DMU without any such form of deception; and by having goods facilities on the traverser sections there's the possibility of a bit of shunting using the scenic and non-scenic lines as sidings. For further interest look out for some examples of short main line trains; a steam locomotive pulling a failed diesel perhaps, a pair of HST power cars en-route from maintenance, a Class 47 and an inspection saloon etc.

At a glance

- **Comprises a main line station with goods facilities.**
- **Employs deceptive use of mainline stock.**
- **Clip on/fold out traverser for extra operational length.**
- **Long narrow design ideal for a shelf situation.**
- **Has scenic section on both traversers to increase shunting interest.**

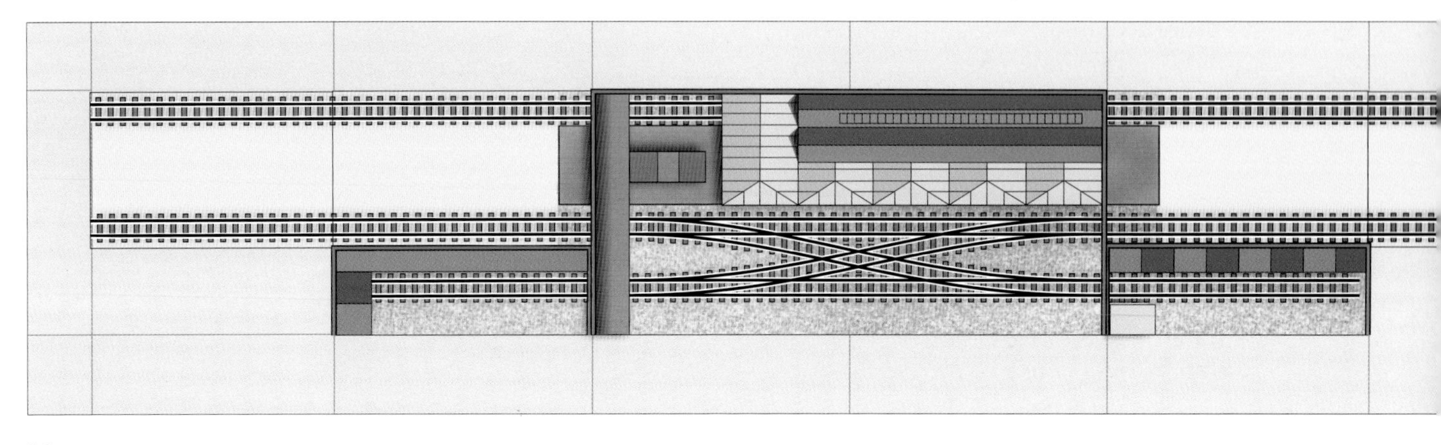

There are elements from both Berwick-upon-Tweed (right) and Penrith (lower right) in this micro-layout design. Comparison between illustration and photographs shows that I have utilised the covered footbridge and canopy from the former, and the retaining wall and overall roof from the latter, both as a focal point for the layout.

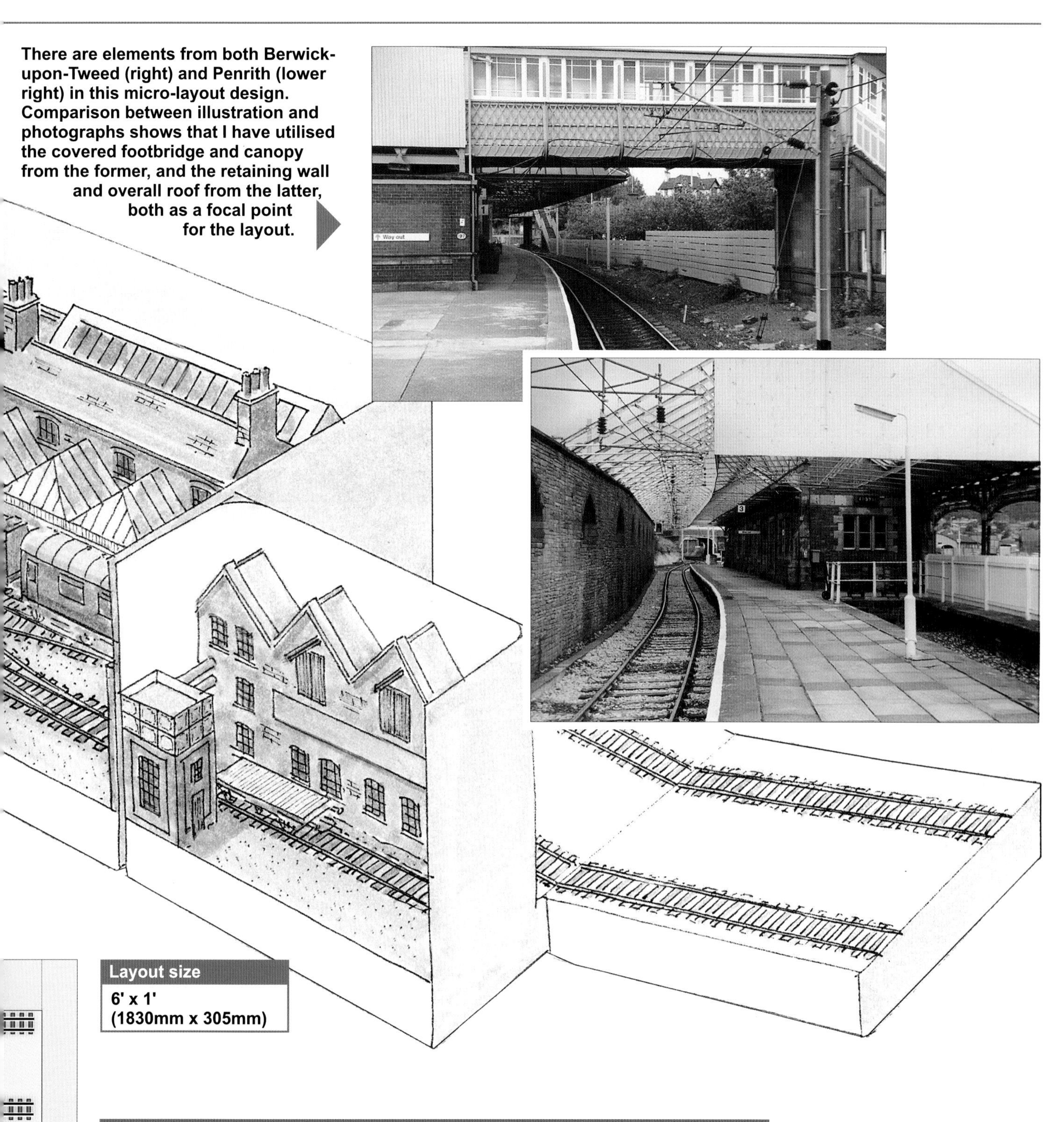

Layout size

6' x 1'
(1830mm x 305mm)

Want to know more?

- **In part, this design takes its inspiration from Penrith and Berwick stations which are on the national rail system.**

Retro Railcar

Inspired by Bere Alston in Devon

A micro-branch line with space saved by the use of hidden non-scenic kick back sidings. The proposed model takes considerable inspiration from the station at Bere Alston as it was in BR ownership although some significant features have been altered, in particular the main road and rail bridge and the direction of the two sidings, otherwise the main changes are in overall compression.

Short trains go hand-in-hand with micro-layouts and therefore single railcars as shown in the illustration together with others like the Dapol Park Royal and Silver Fox AC diesel railbuses are ideal. A short wheel base tank engine or diesel shunter with an appropriate selection of goods wagons would complete the stock list.

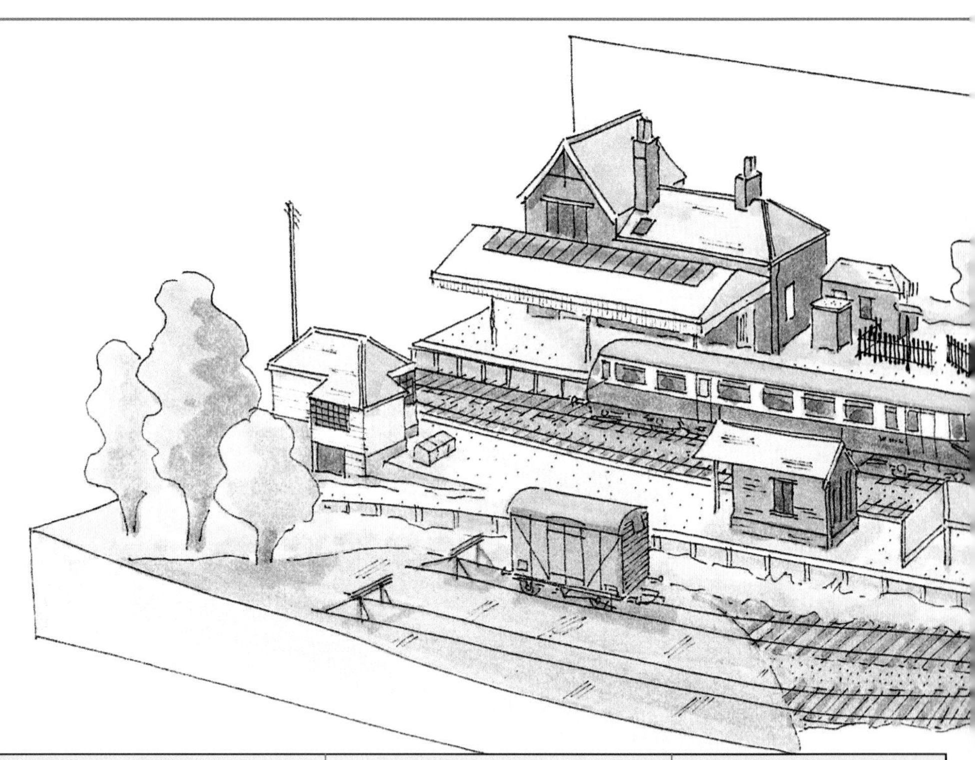

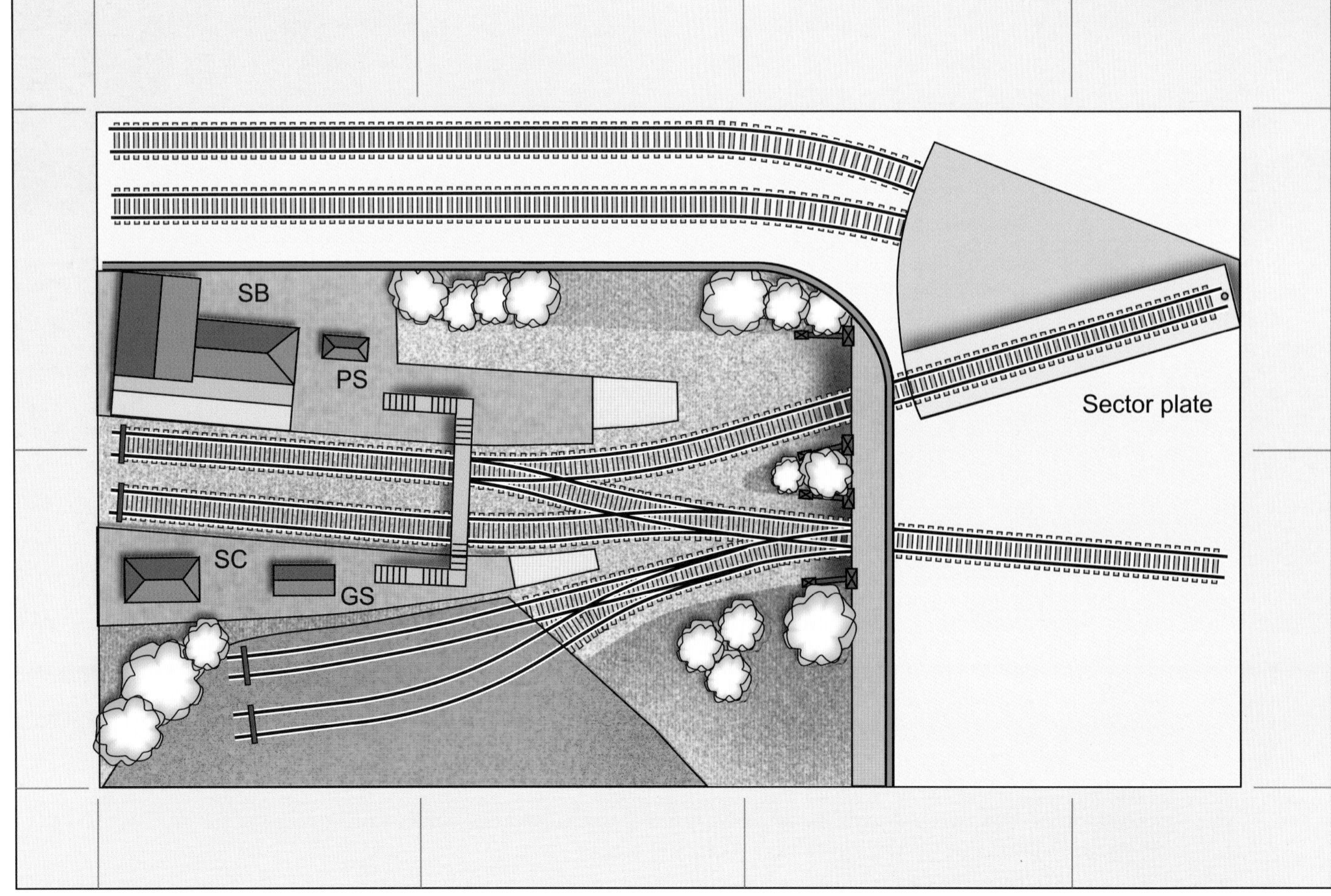

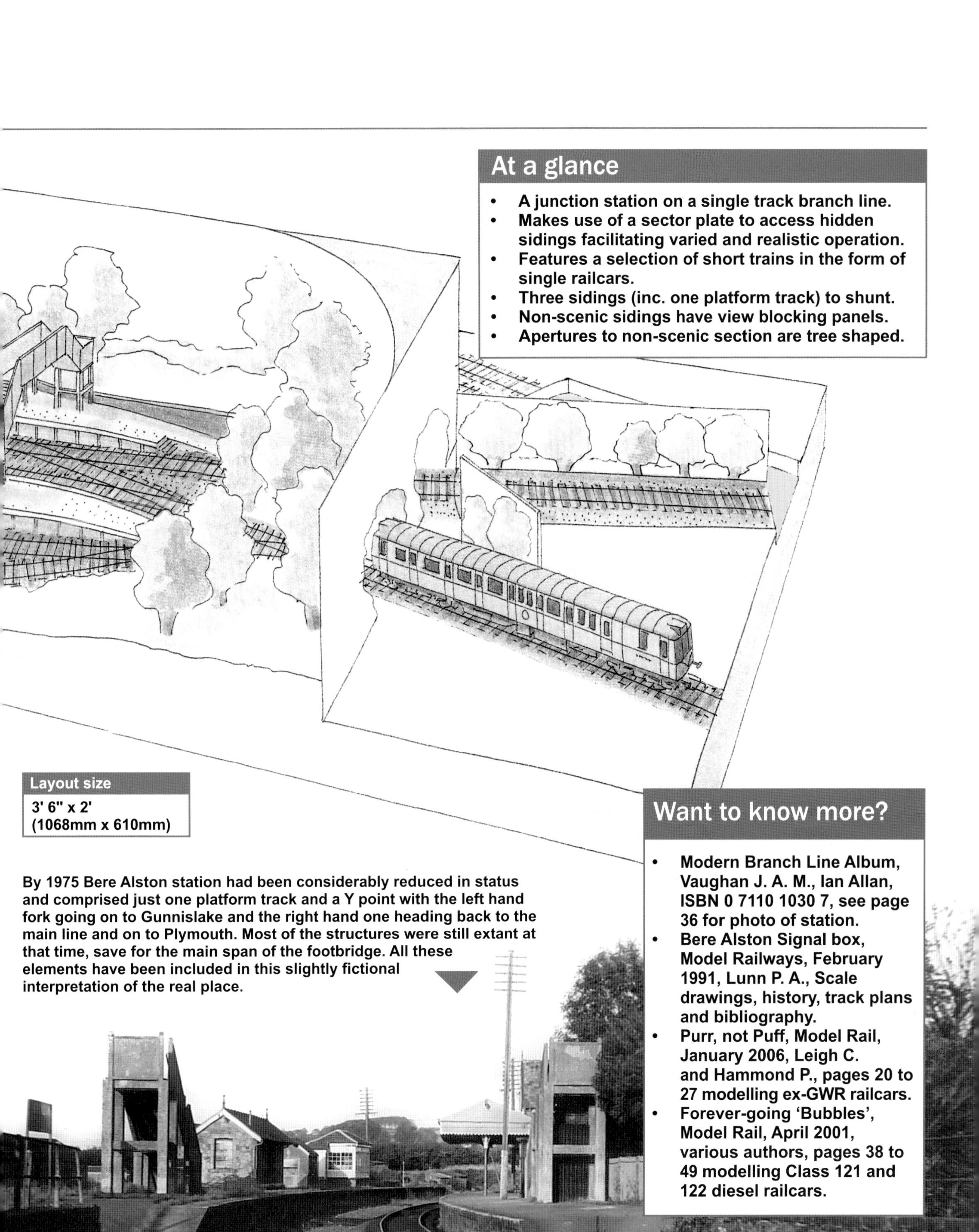

At a glance

- A junction station on a single track branch line.
- Makes use of a sector plate to access hidden sidings facilitating varied and realistic operation.
- Features a selection of short trains in the form of single railcars.
- Three sidings (inc. one platform track) to shunt.
- Non-scenic sidings have view blocking panels.
- Apertures to non-scenic section are tree shaped.

Layout size

3' 6" x 2'
(1068mm x 610mm)

By 1975 Bere Alston station had been considerably reduced in status and comprised just one platform track and a Y point with the left hand fork going on to Gunnislake and the right hand one heading back to the main line and on to Plymouth. Most of the structures were still extant at that time, save for the main span of the footbridge. All these elements have been included in this slightly fictional interpretation of the real place.

Want to know more?

- Modern Branch Line Album, Vaughan J. A. M., Ian Allan, ISBN 0 7110 1030 7, see page 36 for photo of station.
- Bere Alston Signal box, Model Railways, February 1991, Lunn P. A., Scale drawings, history, track plans and bibliography.
- Purr, not Puff, Model Rail, January 2006, Leigh C. and Hammond P., pages 20 to 27 modelling ex-GWR railcars.
- Forever-going 'Bubbles', Model Rail, April 2001, various authors, pages 38 to 49 modelling Class 121 and 122 diesel railcars.

Bembridge

An easy Micro based on an Isle of Wight prototype

The right hand half of this design captures much of the now closed Isle of Wight prototype at Bembridge whereas the left hand half is a fictitious device to hide the small fiddle yard.

As an alternative to scratch building a turntable you may wish to use either a Peco N gauge or HOm turntable, which both appear to share the same size well. I suspect it's quite possible to fit OO track on to both and flush board the well with Wills or similar sheet material. Whatever your choice, there's an excellent photo in Paul Atterbury's book, Discovering Britain's Lost Railways, of the boarded turntable together with O2 Class locomotive No.14 Fishbourne being turned.

I've kept the overall layout as a very simple rural design, with a fiddle yard where a Peco Loco-Lift would be used to release locos. This process removes the requirement of complicated wiring and indeed the skill to produce a traverser.

All the structures can be produced using readily available components in the Wills, Ratio and Peco ranges: even the trees could be bought in if need be.

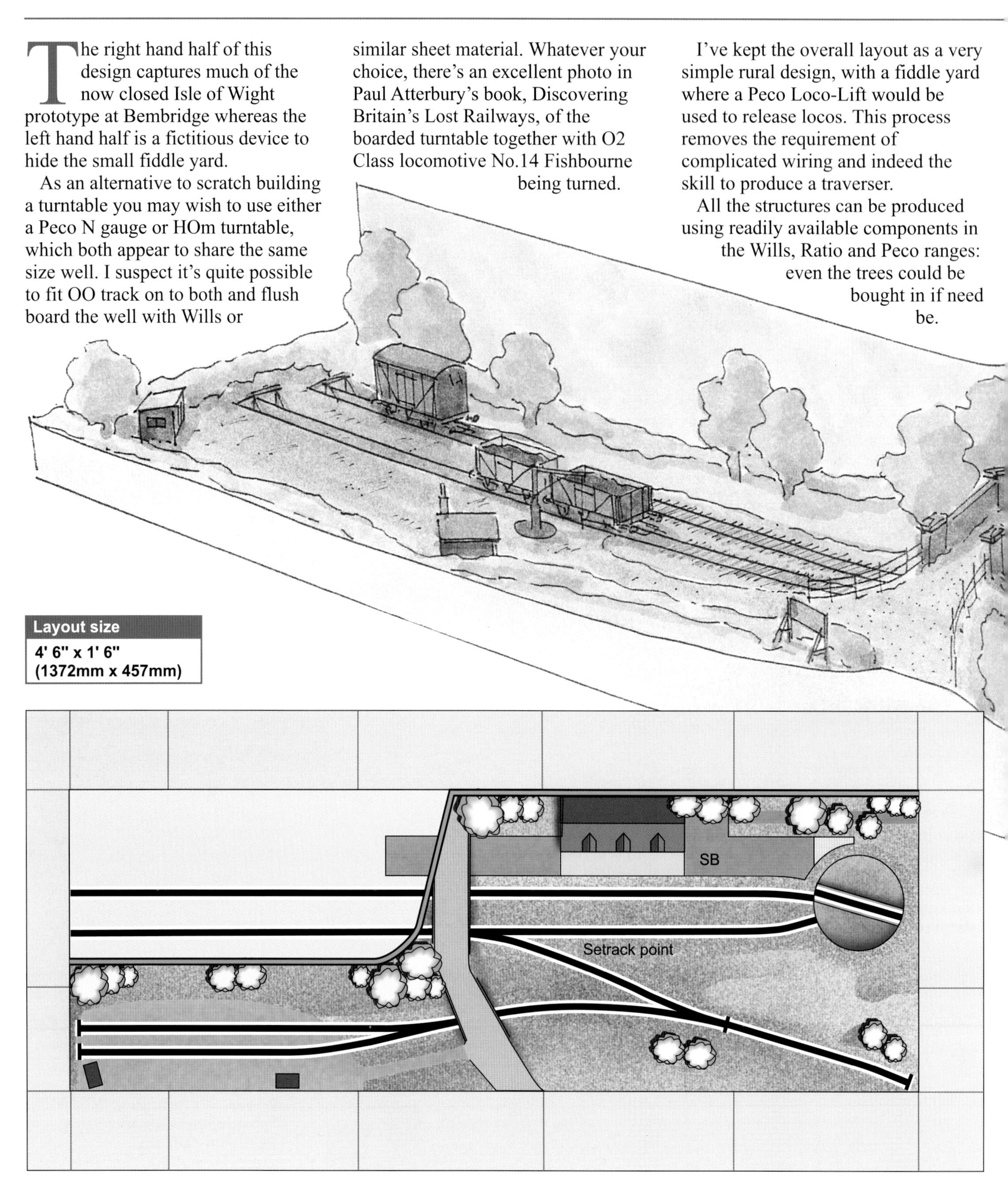

Layout size
4' 6" x 1' 6" (1372mm x 457mm)

Want to know more?

- **Isle of Wight Steam Railway:**
  iwsteamrailway.co.uk
- **Isle of Wight Railways, Pomeroy C. A., Past and Present Publishing, ISBN 1 85895 123 2.**
- **Discovering Britain's Lost Railways, Atterbury P., AA Publishing, see pages 62 - 63 for a large detailed photo of the turntable.**
- **A small turntable in OO, Railway Modeller, January 2006, Hoekstra G. M., page 44.**

At a glance

- **Layout has simple storage sidings using Peco Loco-Lift for run round.**
- **Uses short turntable instead of points to reduce length.**
- **Uses a sharp radius Peco Setrack point to direct siding line away from main overbridge.**

Snibston

A micro-exhibit with potential for extending

This is the second of two layouts (see Barrow Hill) designed not only as a micro-layout but also as an exhibition layout and in this case, recognizing that whilst there might not be much space at home there could be considerable space at the local exhibition! That said, the main unit is self-contained and can be operated as such whilst the extensions are narrow and should be of a length to fit available transport. It is intended these would be supported on a weighted 'A' frame at suitable intervals.

The layout is typical of many colliery lines but takes particular inspiration from the preserved railway at Snibston Discovery Park. Here you will find a wonderful, if somewhat small collection of steam and diesel shunters, together with a range of well battered wagons.

The railway at Snibston Discovery Park has a mix of views, some appear contrived, like the station (new build) and the signal box (moved from another site), whilst others; the pit head and industrial units, still look natural in their original setting. These latter structures form the basis of this layout and are arranged as the focal point of the model. Note the subtle colours where even the light blue bridge has faded sufficiently to be in harmony. Lots of atmosphere with grass growing between the track, rusting wagons, lifted railway line: essential detail for any model railway, but of paramount importance to the micro-layout.

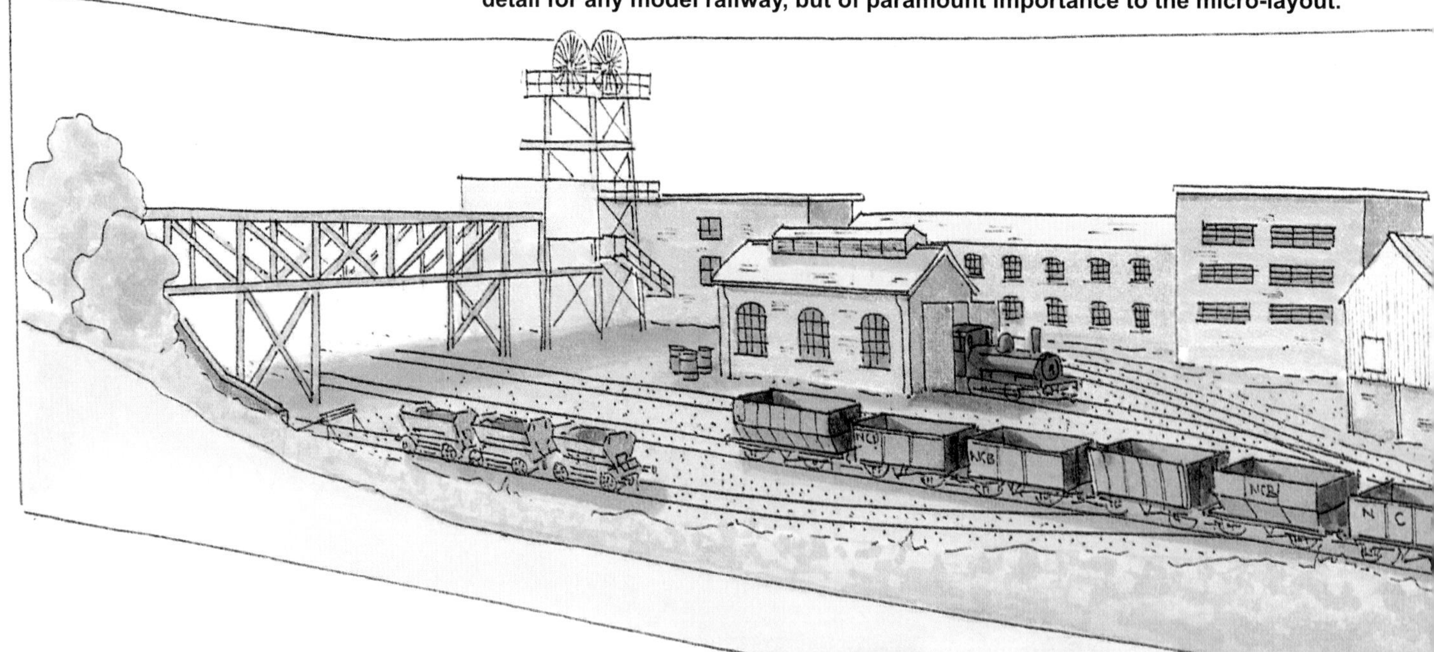

At a glance

- **Small size, self contained, home based layout with micro-extensions (see plan opposite) for exhibition use.**
- **Industrial setting.**
- **Design based on easily accessed prototype in Leicestershire.**

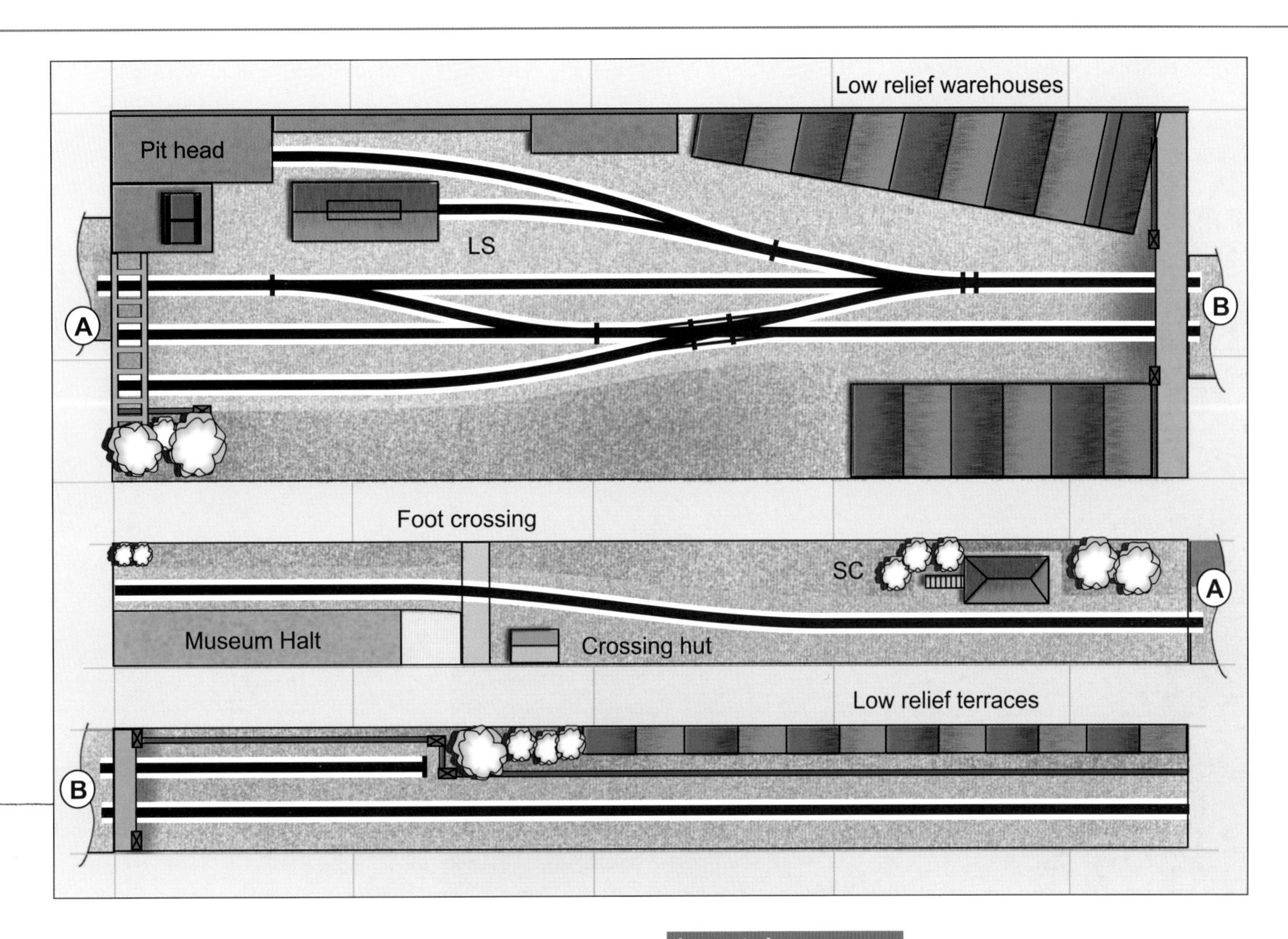

Layout size
4' 6" x 1' 6" (1372mm x 457mm)

Want to know more?

- **Snibston Discovery Park:**
  leics.gov.uk/index/community/museums
- **Instant Industrials - Moving on from Thomas® 1, Lunn P. A., Railway Modeller, November 2006, pages 700 to 702. An article on how to change items from the Hornby Thomas® range into industrial locos.**
- **Industrial Railways in Colour, Booth A., Irwell Press, ISBN 1-903266-14-9.**
- **Industrial Steam, Ian Allan Publishing, various, ISBN 0 7110 2230 5.**
- **Industrial Railway Society:**
  irsociety.co.uk

Frome

Operating through trains

Like the plan on page 38, this design has a facility to represent through trains, albeit only short ones. It uses a single line traverser (at the right hand end) to return stock back via a hidden return line, though a Peco Loco-Lift would work equally well if the station building was left open-ended. Clearly this process is only for single railcars, a light engine or a shunter and a couple of wagons. The traverser is scenically masked by a Brunel style overall roof. Additionally, there are three sidings to shunt at the front of the layout representing an oil depot as per the prototype at Frome, but now long since demolished. To the rear of the layout is a single siding into the old goods shed portrayed in use by Ben Chairs, also as it was on the prototype.

Although Frome station is still on the national rail network it has changed considerably since the time of my photographic surveys of 1979 and 1984.

An overall roof on any layout is a great way to hide any deception that's going on underneath, such as in this case, a hidden traverser. Here a Class 33 passes through on a Weymouth service.

Layout size
6' x 2' 1"
(1830mm x 635mm)

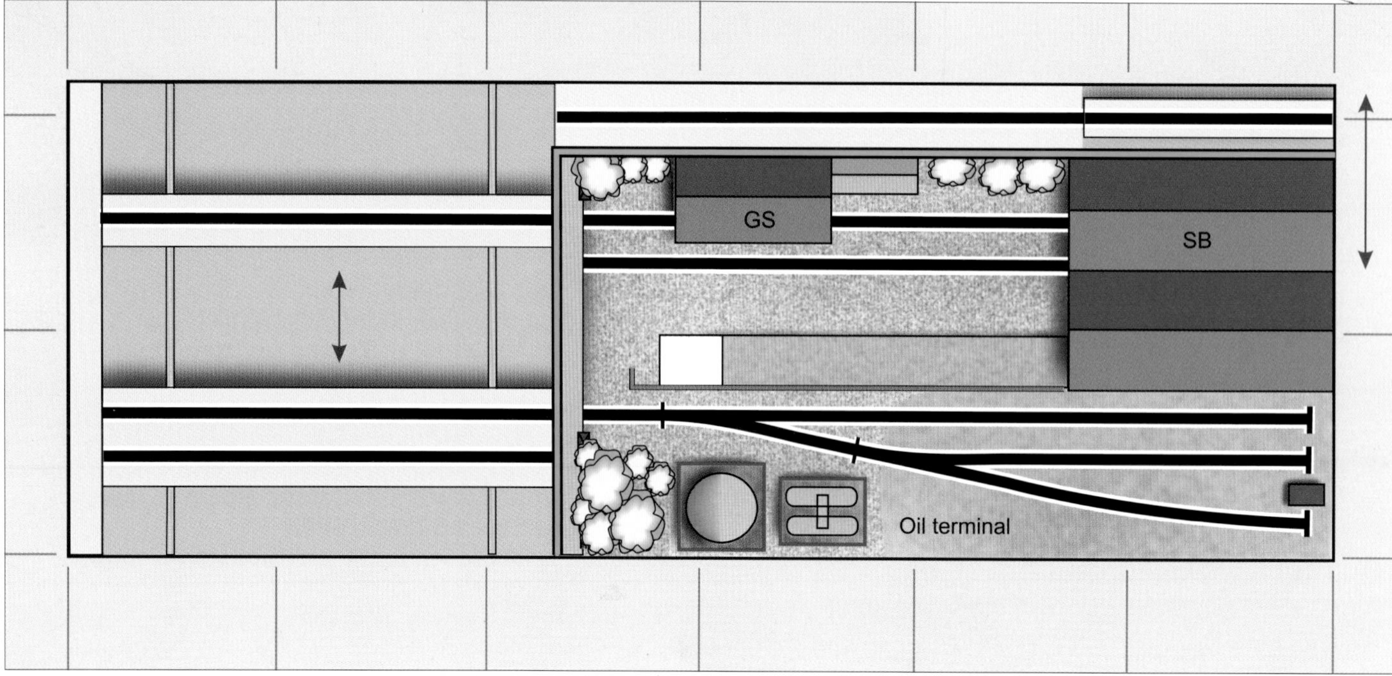

Want to know more?

- A Historical Survey of Selected Great Western Stations, Clark R. H., pages 74 to 80. Includes historical text, track plans and several useful photographs.
- Rolling Stock Recognition 2: BR and Private Owner Wagons, Marsden C. J., Ian Allan, ISBN0 7110 1403 5, page 110 photo and brief description of PVB Ben Chairs wagon.
- Liquid on Rails, Bartlett P., Model Rail, September 2001, pages 22 to 27 an article on four wheel tank wagons and how to model them.

At a glance

- Short through trains are handled via hidden return line.
- Layout has four sidings to shunt and although shown as an oil and chair depot, there is no reason why alternative traffic could be handled.
- The layout needs a main traverser on left hand side beyond the road overbridge, which I would recommend is at least 91.5cm (3') long.

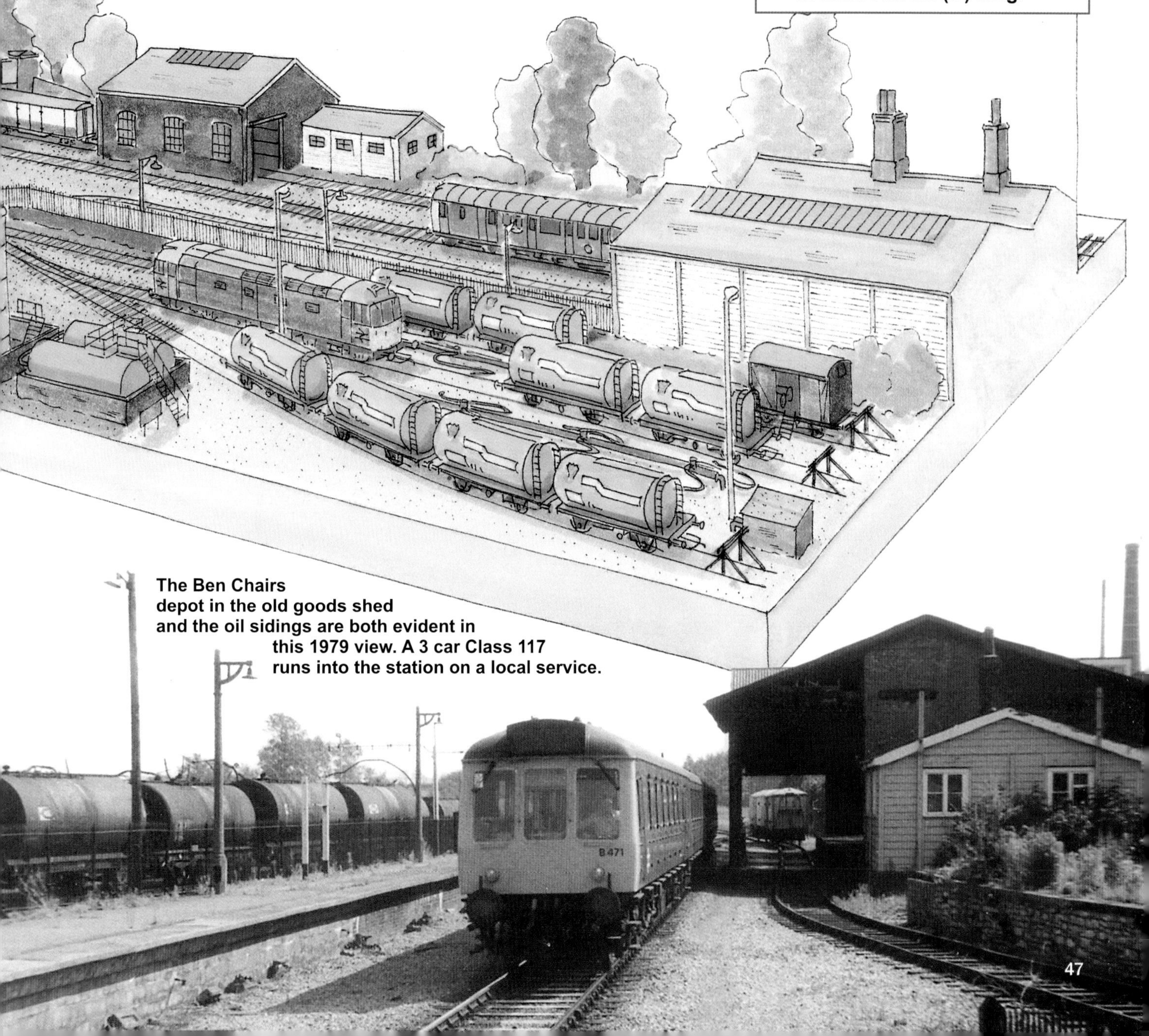

The Ben Chairs depot in the old goods shed and the oil sidings are both evident in this 1979 view. A 3 car Class 117 runs into the station on a local service.

Hide and See

A West Yorkshire based urban scheme

This scheme combines structure modelling with quite intensive operational potential. Structures on the upper level are however applied to a formula rather than at random. Buildings in the front row are modelled at full relief with half and low relief behind. A 3D representation of buildings should be painted on the 2D backscene to complete the overall impression of a city or townscape. Furthermore, particular attention needs to be paid to streets that run from front to back. These must not be allowed to run unblocked from the retaining wall to the backscene or the change between 2D and 3D may appear clumsy. The solution is to view block the street at the half or low relief line. Ideally this would be a building but it could be a combination of things including a

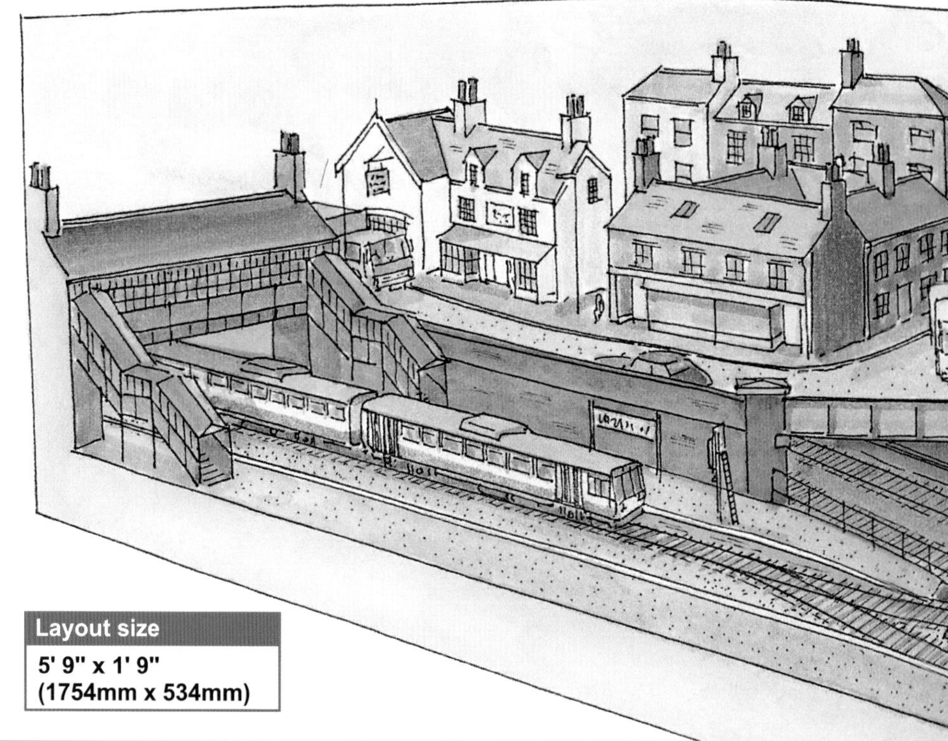

Layout size

5' 9" x 1' 9"
(1754mm x 534mm)

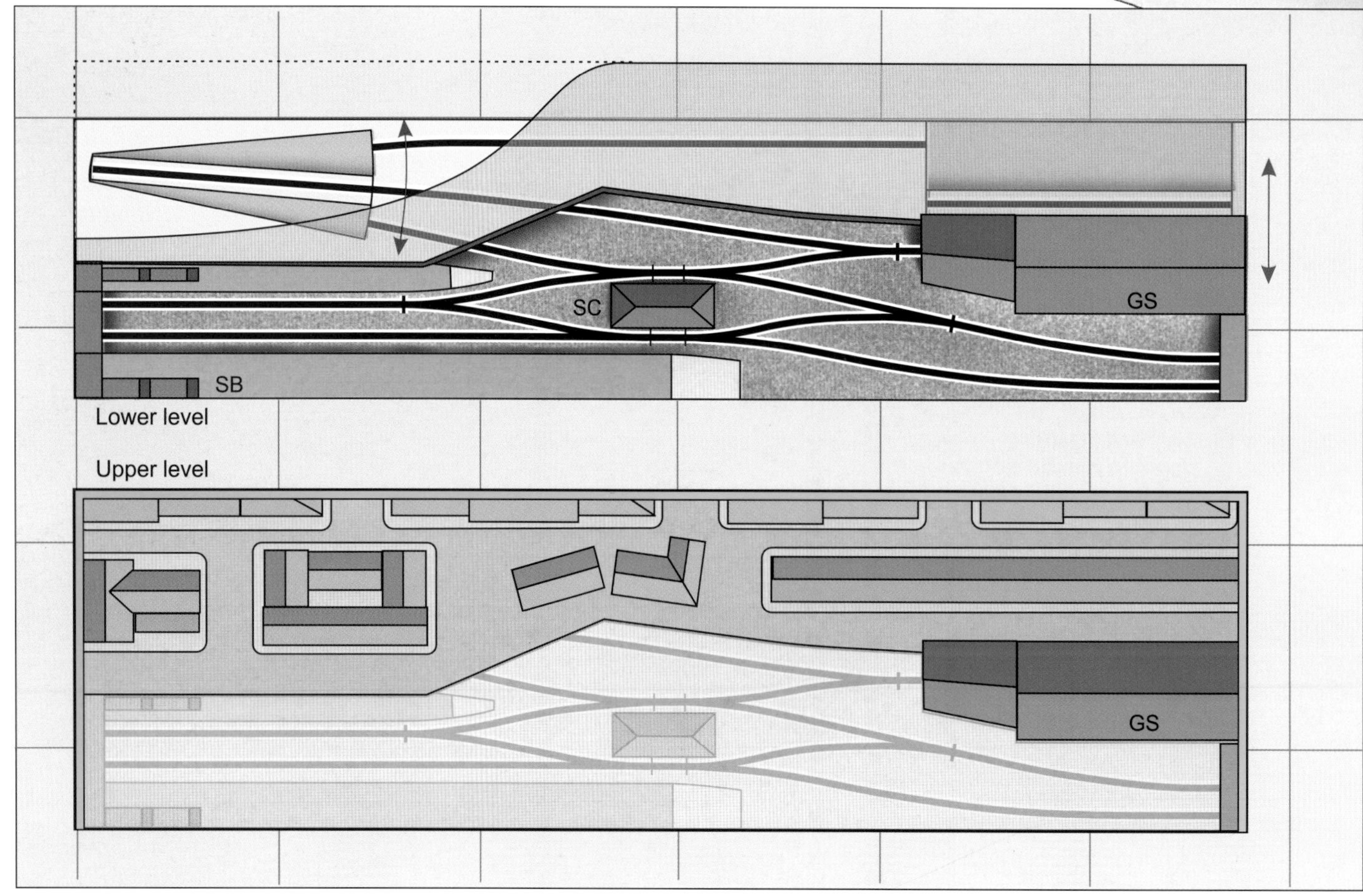

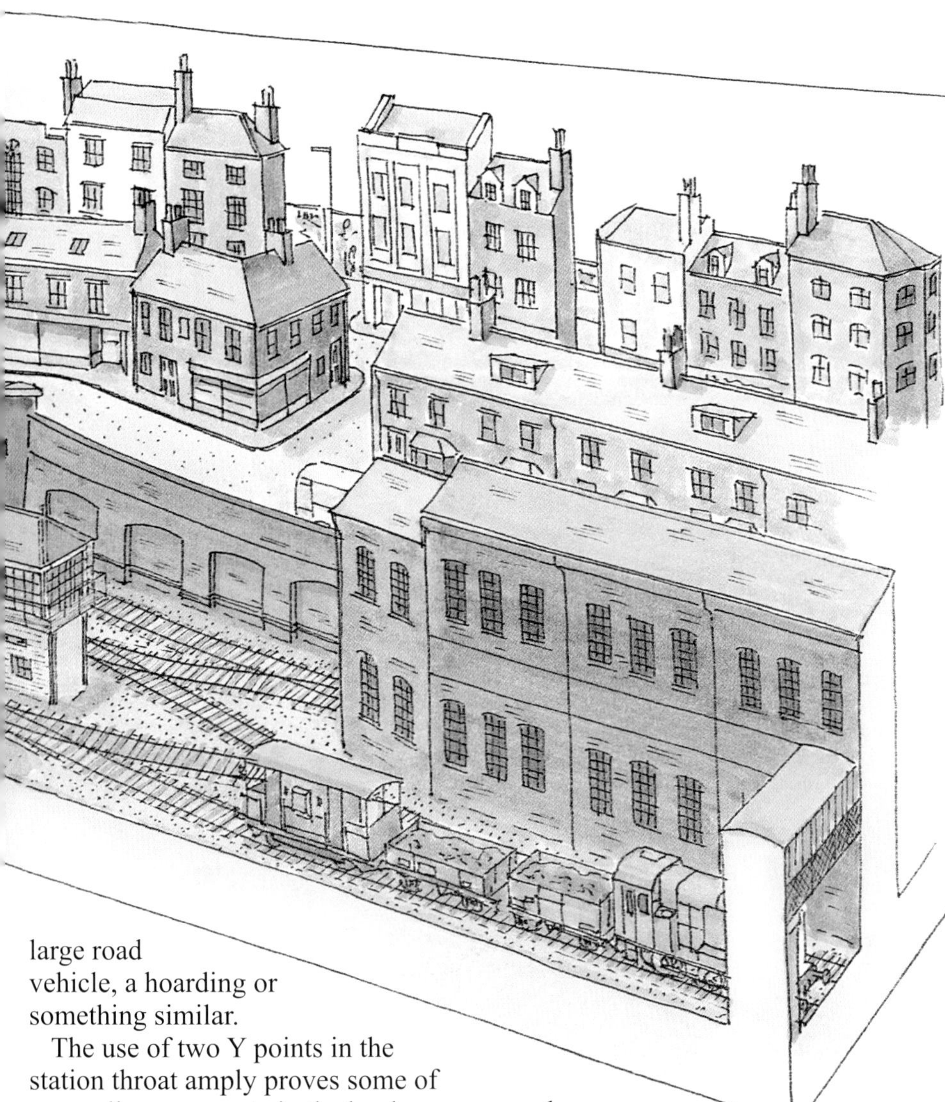

At a glance

- Sector plate and traverser allows for simulation of through trains.
- High-level town scene used to hide storage sidings.
- Model as a semi-disused ex-main line station which explains the presence of short passenger trains and modest shunting.
- Relies on the length quality of the Hornby two car Class 142 Pacer unit.

Want to know more?

- The layout takes inspiration from W. Yorks prototypes including Wakefield Kirkgate (station), Guiseley/Ilkley (signal box) and Huddersfield (warehouse).
- First Steps in Railway Modelling, Ellis C., Midland Publishing, ISBN 1 85780 066 4. Pages 29 and 30 give an account on sector plate construction.

large road vehicle, a hoarding or something similar.

The use of two Y points in the station throat amply proves some of my earlier comments in the book on track usage. Whilst a double slip might be slightly shorter, quite graceful and perhaps a little more railwaylike, the angle, especially with larger units is too gentle and in the case of this design would result in the track behind the warehouse hitting the end of it instead. The same would happen with the track to the sector plate which would hit the bridge upright instead of passing under the girder; most unsatisfactory. The curve off from a pair of Y points is much sharper and allows us to meet design requirements whilst looking somewhat like a double slip and perhaps more importantly providing all the necessary functions.

Operation includes through trains from sector plate to traverser and return, passenger trains running into the station from the traverser or reversing in from the sector plate and of course several sidings to shunt.

Guiseley station was in immaculate condition with this great example of an oversailing signal box when photographed over twenty years ago. The box design is suitable for the restricted space inside the tiny loop of this plan.

Across the Diagonal

Eye level viewing with forced perspective

Inspired by Andrew Knights' excellent designing skills featured in a recent Railway Modeller article, this layout endeavours to pack in as much as possible by having track across the diagonal on two levels together with the addition of some TT gauge (3mm:ft scale) to enhance perspective.

The key to visual success is taking an almost eye level viewpoint for operation; where the foreground is modelled in OO and the rear, glimpsed through archways under the main girder bridge, is where the TT gauge is used. Viewing the rear of the layout from above, behind the high level track, will almost certainly spoil the illusion of depth. Similarly, my proposal to model the line from the OO section at the front to the TT turntable at a reducing scale, is purely for visual effect: clearly no stock will ever be able to run on it!

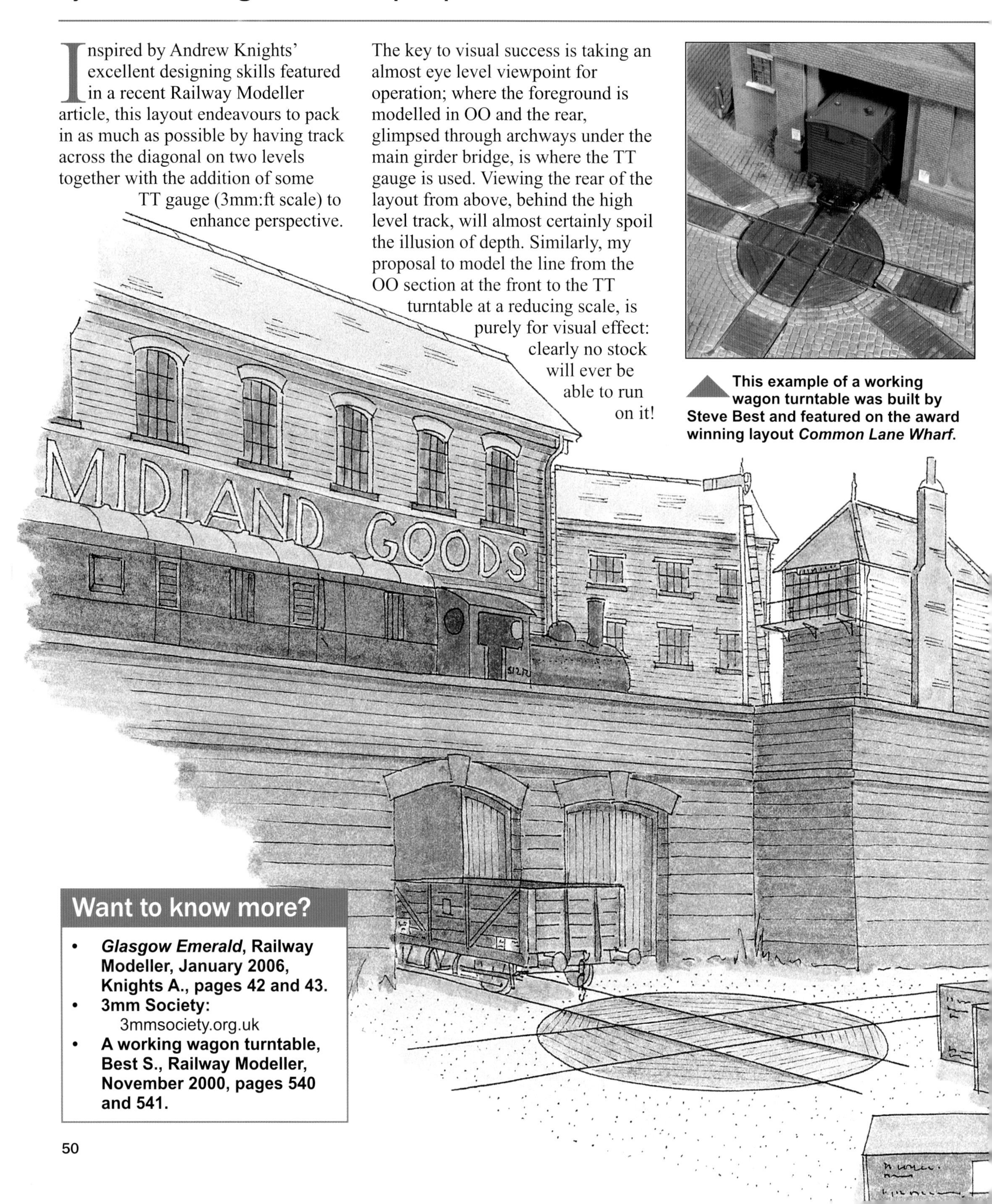

This example of a working wagon turntable was built by Steve Best and featured on the award winning layout *Common Lane Wharf*.

Want to know more?

- ***Glasgow Emerald*, Railway Modeller, January 2006, Knights A., pages 42 and 43.**
- **3mm Society:** 3mmsociety.org.uk
- **A working wagon turntable, Best S., Railway Modeller, November 2000, pages 540 and 541.**

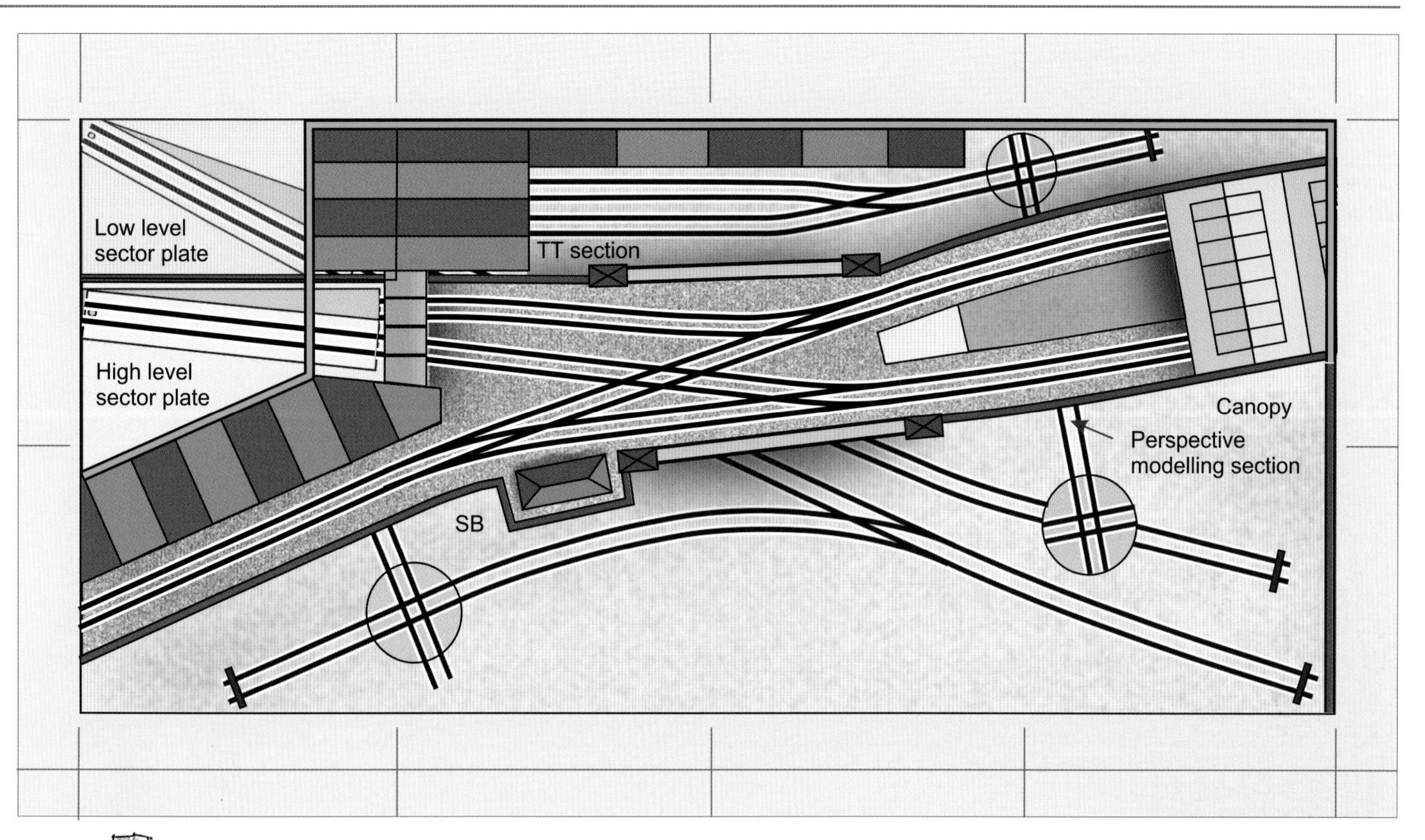

Layout size

**4' x 1' 10"
(1220mm x 559mm)**

At a glance

- **Extra running length for the available space by placing tracks across the diagonal and on two levels.**
- **Layout to be modelled in OO at the front and on the upper level. The rear lower section to be modelled in TT enhancing perspective - this section is only visible by peering through the lower level arches.**
- **Perspective modelling used between both wagon turntables and through archway to create the illusion of greater distance.**
- **Has a challenging mixed gauge (OO & TT) sector plate at lower level.**

Bolsover

Double sided viewing

I stated in the introduction that you need to be careful not to put too much track into a micro-layout or it will look busy and over-crowded. Like all statements there's always going to be an exception and this is it. Start by looking at the track plan based on Coalite's Coking works at Bolsover and you'll see what I mean, nearly every inch of baseboard has a piece of track on it and as such the 2D footprint image of the layout is already starting to send out warning bells. The solution is in the 3D interpretation. By making a composite design of the prototype's main structures, most of which are elevated above ground level on girder stilts and placing them as a divider slightly diagonally down the middle of the baseboard, you effectively split the layout in two. Not in the way a solid backscene with a printed scenic image on both sides would divide a baseboard into two layouts, but one where you can see parts of both sides at the same time. As a result the design looks less crowded, certainly as far as track is concerned.

Layout size

4' x 1' 10"
(1220mm x 559mm)

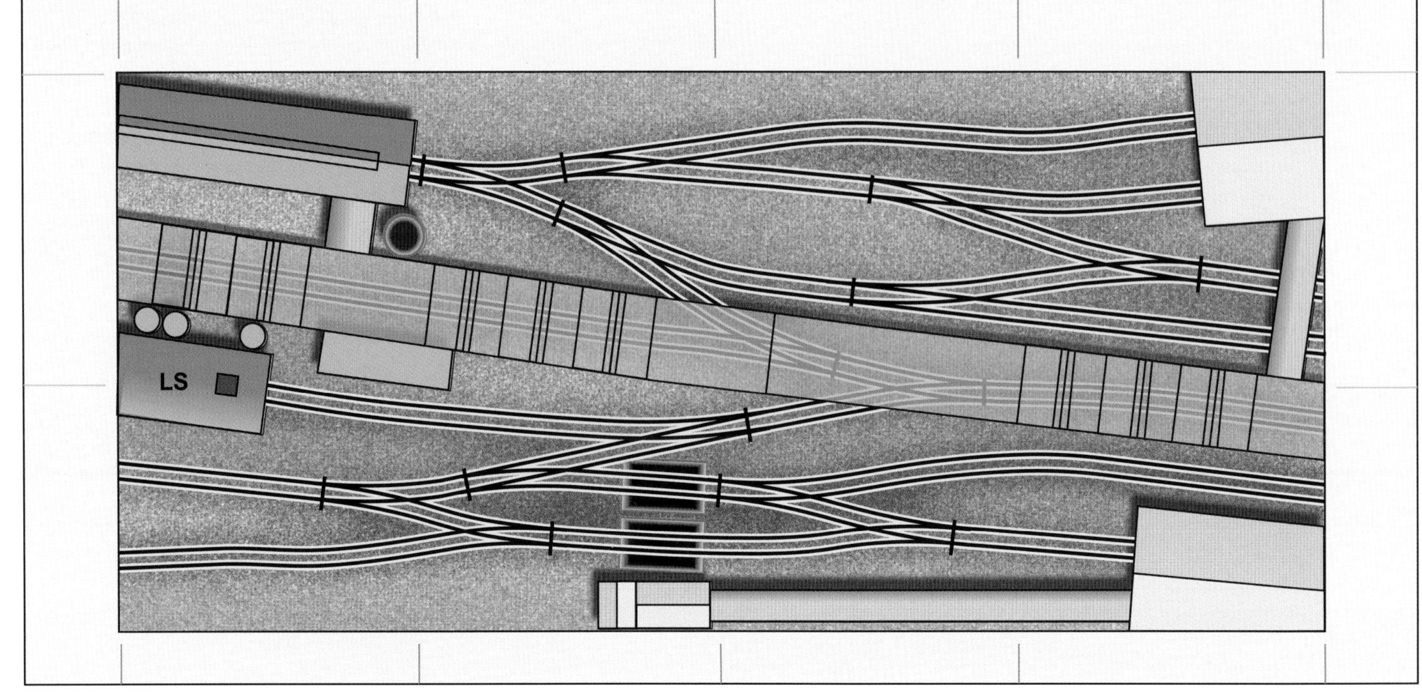

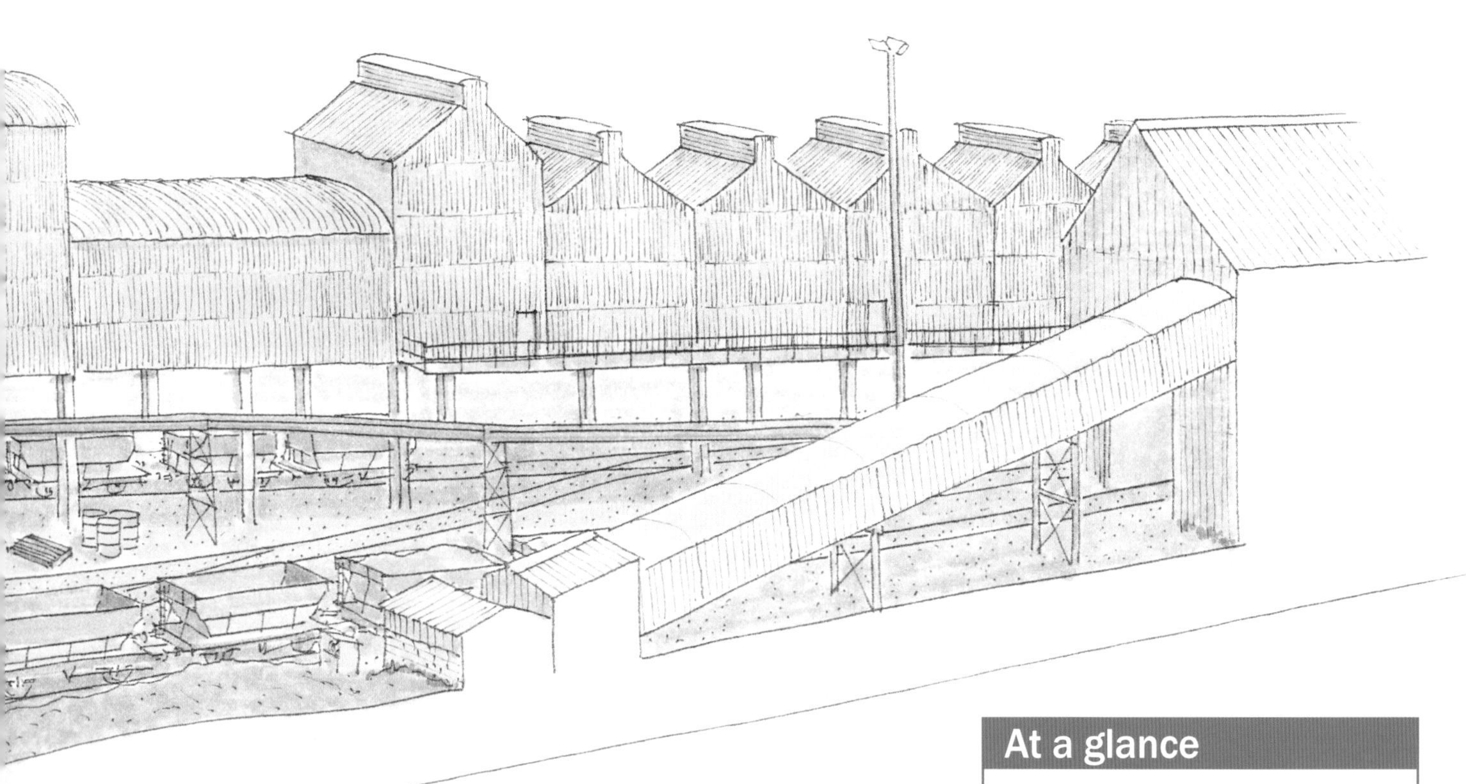

This loco workshop at Coalite Works, despite being only of basic brick construction with a cast concrete roof, is literally covered with interesting features worth modelling; vents, pipes, safety rail, safety ladder, roof mounted pipework and so on. On the ground are further bits and pieces: all-in-all a huge amount of detailing that would need attending to.

At a glance

- **High track content.**
- **Buildings used as a backscene, partly 'see through' to divide one layout into two more intimate dioramas.**
- **The scheme was developed using food containers and household packaging in the design process (see actual method on page 25).**
- **Design facilitates presence of mainline locomotives.**

Want to know more?

- **Industrial Railway Society has a variety of entries referring to Coalite's Bolsover Coking Plant:**
  irsociety.co.uk
- **The Sentinel shunter is available as a plastic kit from Knightwing. It can be motorised with a suitable chassis pack available from Branchlines.**

Multi-Choice Modular Micro

Based on the Bervie Branch in N. E. Scotland

Double sided backscenes, not necessarily down the centre, are a great way of doubling up running length in a given space. In this instance the idea is that a main baseboard frame is built which includes both 'fiddle ends' (one is a turntable and one is a traverser) as seen in Fig 1. The scenic modules could either be built as back-to-back station pairs on one board 2' 2" x 2', or as individual stations on 2' 2" x 1' boards. The design could therefore have a choice of any two stations from four. As an extra bonus, if the traversers were built as modules as well, then one could be removed and a longer board 3' 5" containing a terminus station (Fig 2.) could substituted, giving a total of six different modules for one main frame.

Some accurate and consistent building skills are required to maintain uniformity which will underpin the multi-choice options. Longer term the turntable, traverser and sub-frame could be used for all manner of designs.

As it stands, trains are limited in length to that of the turntable at 30cm (1' 00"). Nevertheless, there is a possibility of considerable variety like those shown elsewhere in this book, together with light engines. Modern modellers might wish to use single railcars and Class 04, 06, or 08 shunters for branch freight traffic.

Want to know more?

- **Modelling Scotland's Railways, I. Futers, Santona Publications. ISBN 0-9538448-8-9. Page 71: St Cyrus station and building drawing.**

Layout size

4' 6" x 2' overall (1220mm x 610mm), each module: 2' 2" x 1' min.

At a glance

- **Allows modelling of a branch line rather than one station or facility.**
- **Multi-choice of design due to uniform size of modules.**
- **Base unit including turntable and traverser can be used for future layouts**
- **Excluding Bervie this design is an 'oval without curves'.**
- **Longer terminus unit as shown in Fig 2. could be made if half of the traverser section was made removable.**
- **Has view blocking non-scenic turntable.**
- **Some scenic treatment of traverser as a view block through bridge aperture.**
- **See also multi-choice mock-ups, on which this scheme is based, page 26.**

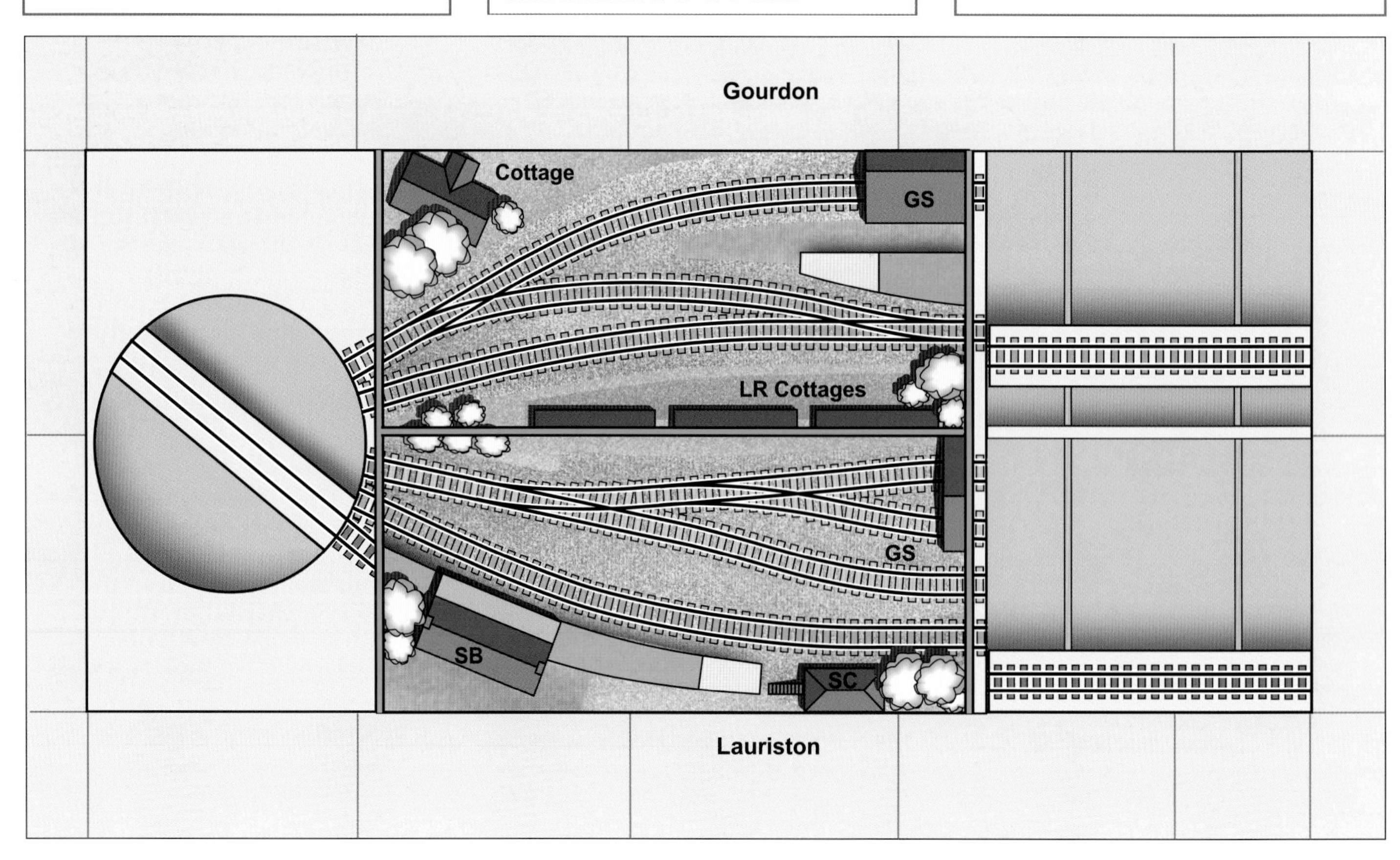

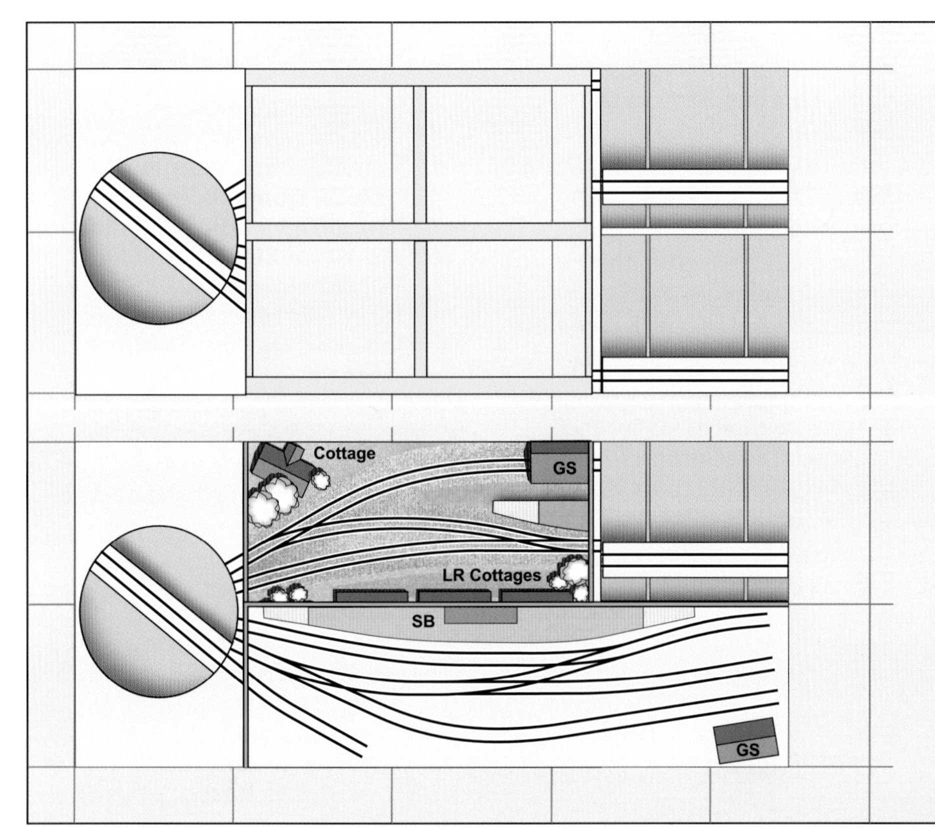

Fig 1. The main baseboard frame constructed from tried and trusted 50mm x 25mm (2" x1") PSE softwood. The turntable and traverser sections should be built on sub-frames of 2" x 1" timber to raise them up to allow clearance for the recessed areas. Each of the modular boards would also be built on a sub-frame so as to simply slide or drop into place. Some plastic Conti-board joiners could be used underneath to keep the tracks aligned.

Fig 2. This shows the possible third configuration in which the traversers are made removable too. A complete board representing a terminus station will now fit in the space as shown in the lower half of the diagram. Likewise the top half could be so treated as well. Note that if the diameter of the turntable was increased, slightly longer trains could be operated without significantly lengthening the layout.

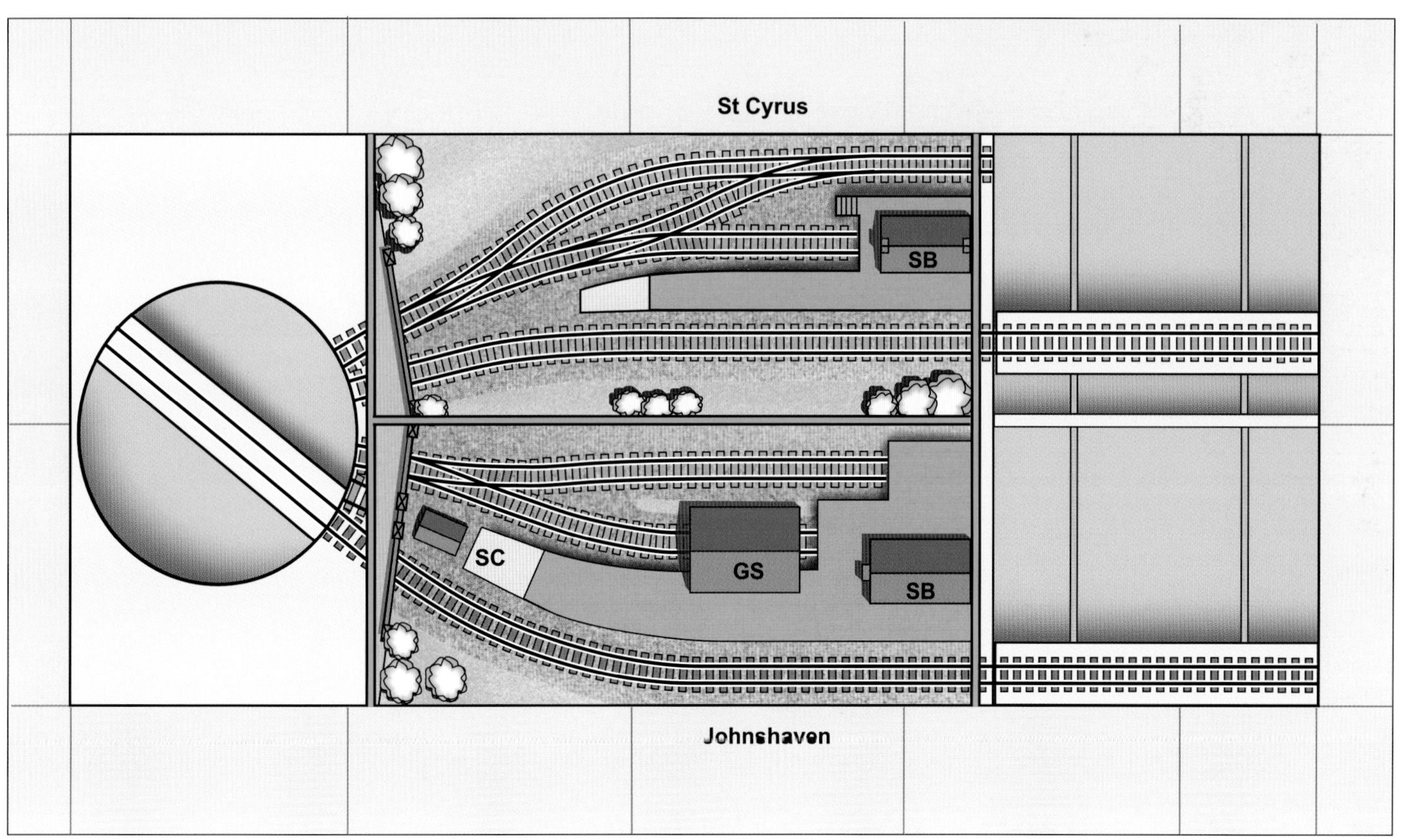

Both Sides Now

Alternative layout views with removable backscene

There's no rhyme or reason to the design process. I find that ideas sometimes come faster than I can write them down which means in these days of elderly forgetfulness I have note pads, scrap paper and drawing kit all over the place and we seldom leave the house without a drawing pad and camera. That said, when I'm not working at railways I often relax by playing the guitar and it's Joni Mitchell's song, the first song I learned as it happens back in the 1960s, of the same name, that inspired this particular idea.

Having a layout where the backscene can be fixed along either side will not increase running length but it will give you twice the view and as such make operation more interesting. It's important to consider scenic treatment in such a way that structures do not impede operation or aesthetics. Therefore you will observe that I have made the hidden sidings accessible from both sides, there is an open and uncluttered space in the middle section and two different view blocks in the form of loco sheds at one end. I think it's best to avoid, for example, a row of relief buildings down one side, as might be found on a traditional one-sided layout which I fear would not only reduce viewing enjoyment but also make activities like manual uncoupling quite tedious.

Want to know more

- **Foxfield Railway:** foxfieldrailway.co.uk
- **Industrial Railways in Colour, Booth A., Irwell Press, ISBN 1-903266-14-9.**
- **Industrial Steam, Ian Allan Publishing, various authors, ISBN 0-7110-2230-5.**
- **Industrial Railway Society:** irsociety.co.uk

At a glance

- **Backscene can be placed on either side of the layout giving two different views.**

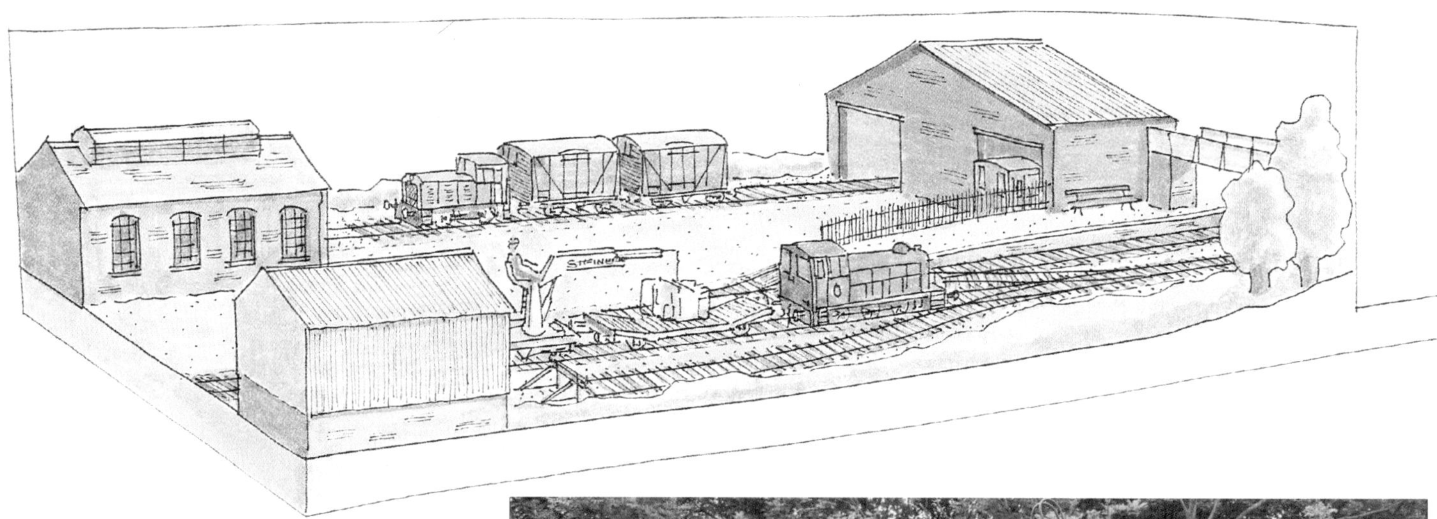

A photograph of a work in progress scene on the Foxfield Railway. This would make a great little feature if you can model and animate it with a moving crane. I have included it on a siding in the artist's impression above. The area is full of small details that all modellers should take note; the generator unit, a modern hydraulic crane fitted to an old railway wagon, wood packing pieces, steel plates and when it comes to attire, what has to be one of the snazziest dressed railway operatives around!

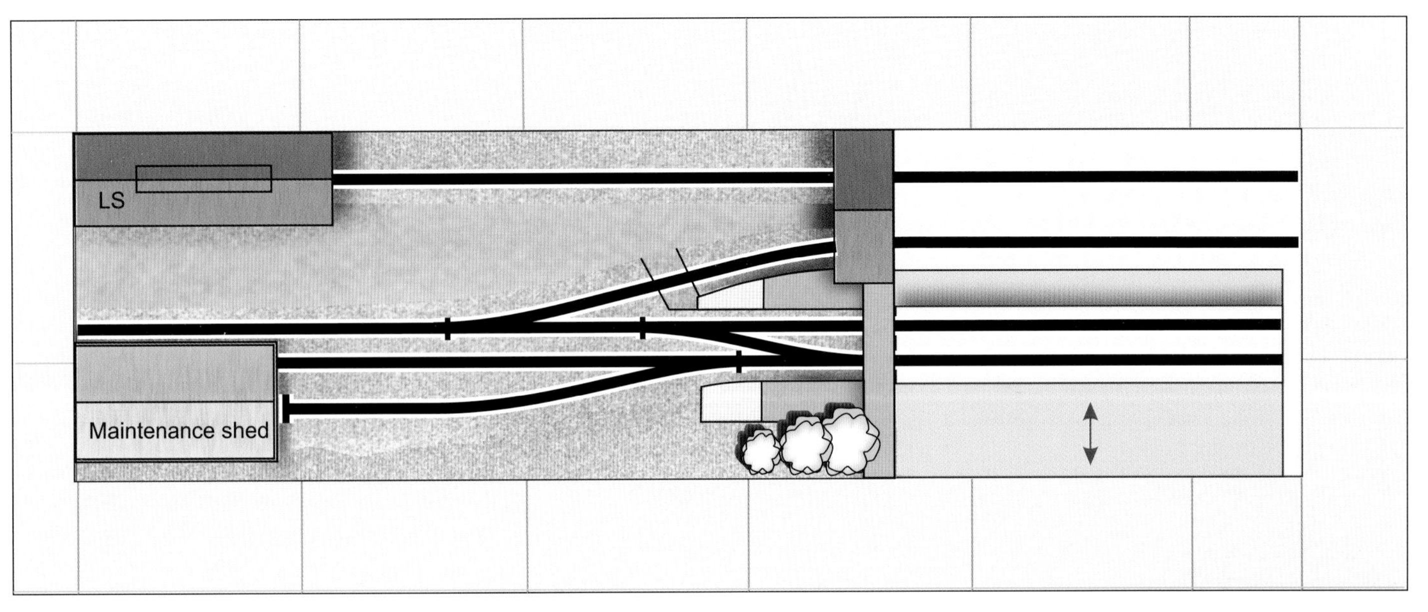

Layout size

**5' 6" x 1' 6"
(1677mm x 457mm)**

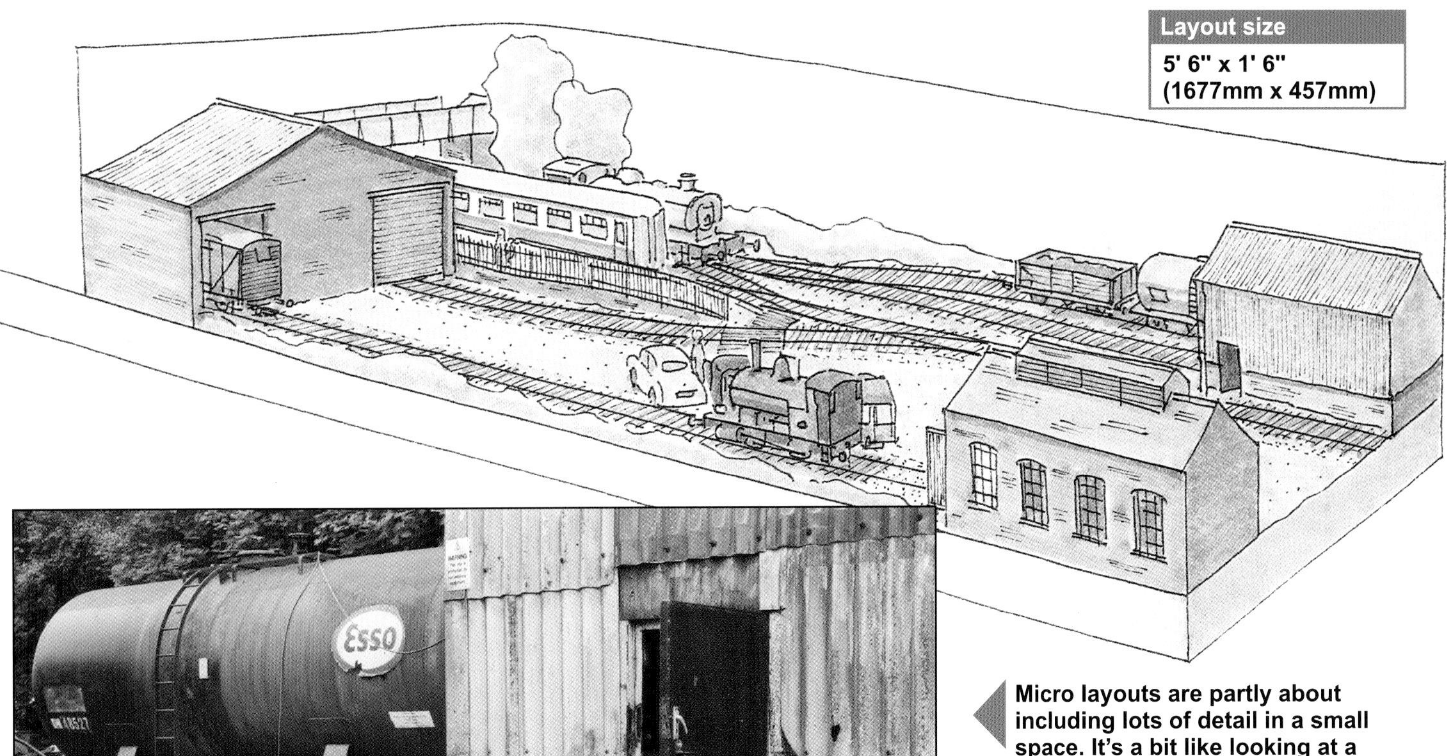

Micro layouts are partly about including lots of detail in a small space. It's a bit like looking at a close-up photograph to see what's going on. I've included this to illustrate that point; Look at the maintenance shed with broken and missing asbestos corrugated sheet, a door with two handles, a sign lent against the wall, various floor surfaces (ash, sleepers, concrete and brick), pipes and cables to the tank wagon and a wooden chock to stop its wheels from moving (presumably if the brakes fail).

Forcing Perspective

Cambrian Coast scene

Probably the greatest skill to develop in designing and building a micro-layout is that of creating something that appears to be more than it actually is. There are many trick and tools, already described, but none will be as stunning as enhanced perspective, if done well. Start with inspiration from the prototype: look at the accompanying photograph of Barmouth Bridge and imagine it to be a model with the DMU in OO in the foreground and the bridge in the distance in N. Now switch to the artist's impression; in the foreground I've suggested a typical ex-Cambrian branch line modelled in OO. The Class 25 is about to collect a solitary mineral wagon, couple up to the brake van and depart off-stage into the non-scenic sidings. Moments later an identical counterpart, purporting to be the same train, but in N gauge, will leave the non-scenic sidings to pass the distant station, collecting wagons on its way to a distant terminus.

To be effective the landmass between both stations will have to be modelled on a reducing scale from OO through HO, TT to N. As such roads will get slightly narrower; trees will reduce in height and so on.

It's a process that will require a number of mock-ups if the outcome is to be convincing and of course, the illusion will need to be viewed at eye level otherwise it's unlikely the eye will be fooled!

Want to know more

- **Perspective on backscenes, Mackintosh A. and Leigh C., Model Rail, Summer Issue 1998, pages 32 to 35, an article about modelling in enhanced and forced perspective.**
- **The Gauge O Guild, Ray J., Railway Modeller, September 2006, page 562, although O gauge, see top left photo.**
- **N Gauge Society:** ngaugesociety.com
- **The Cambrian Lines, Johnson P., Ian Allan, ISBN 0-7110-1400-0.**

A favourite prototype photograph of mine which amply demonstrates the possibility of modelling one scene in two scales. It underpins the micro-layout designer's wish to make a layout appear much more than it really is. In this 1990s view a Class 158 two car unit rounds the tight curve 'twixt Barmouth Bridge and station.

At a glance

- Model of a branch line rather than one station or freight facility.
- Uses enhanced perspective by employing matching train sets; OO at the front and N at the rear.

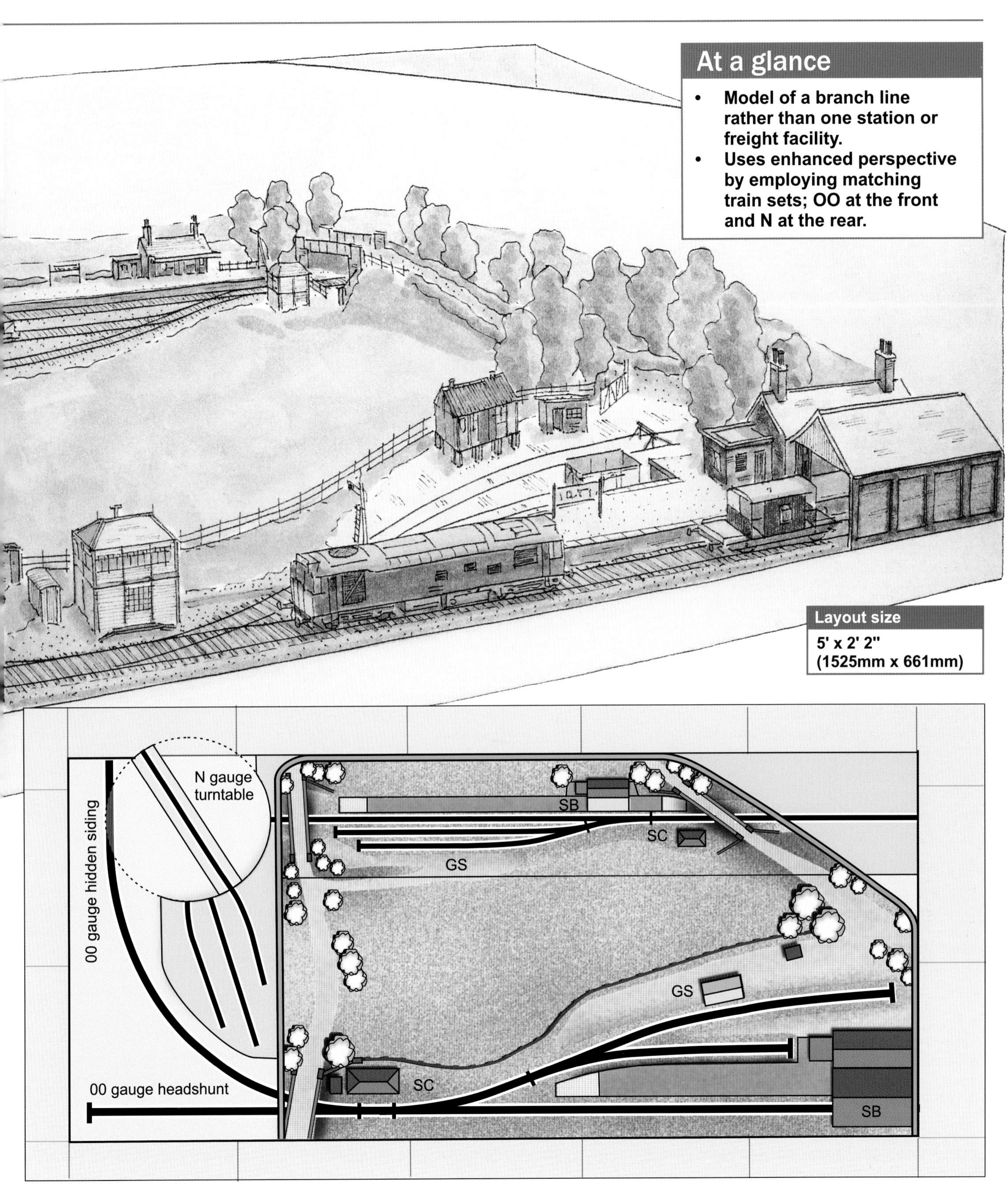

Layout size

5' x 2' 2"
(1525mm x 661mm)

An Inside Out Circle

Creating the *Devonport triangle* dock layout

Take the idea of dividing a circle of track into three segments, turn it inside out on itself and this is what you get. Besides looking more railway-like (if you model dock railways), it takes up slightly less width. Add a sector plate and you have the chance of including some sidings in the central area which of course, is complicated to do on the inside of a circuit of minimum radius curves (Peco or Hornby).

There's no doubting the quality and availability of Peco track components but like all things there are limitations in the breadth of range. If you're unable to scratchbuild track then you will have to cast your net wider, even across the big pond, to buy unusual items like the 90° crossing; one in Code 100 is made by Atlas. However, soon to be introduced (at the time of writing) is a new 90° crossing in the Peco Code 83 range, which can be joined to both Code 100 and Code 75 track without too much difficulty, and thus can be incorporated in this plan, particularly as the sleepers (which will be American HO spacing) will be hidden beneath the inset setts. So the essential item for this plan, and any self respecting dock layout, can soon be acquired easily.

Want to know more

- **Devonport Dockyard Railway, Burkhalter P., Twelveheads Press, ISBN 0-906294-37-1.**
- **The Weymouth Harbour Tramway, Beale G., Wild Swan Publications, ISBN 1-874103-67-4.**
- **Milford Haven docks, OO/HO Setrack Planbook (second edition), Peco Publications and Publicity, see plan 34.**

At a glance

- **Triangular design allows for maximum track in a minimum space and has no 'wasted' corners usually associated with a traditional oval or circle.**
- **Baseboard edge can be used to form dockside.**
- **Uses some American track to provide greater geometric flexibility**
- **Hidden track storage inside central building used as a space saving device.**

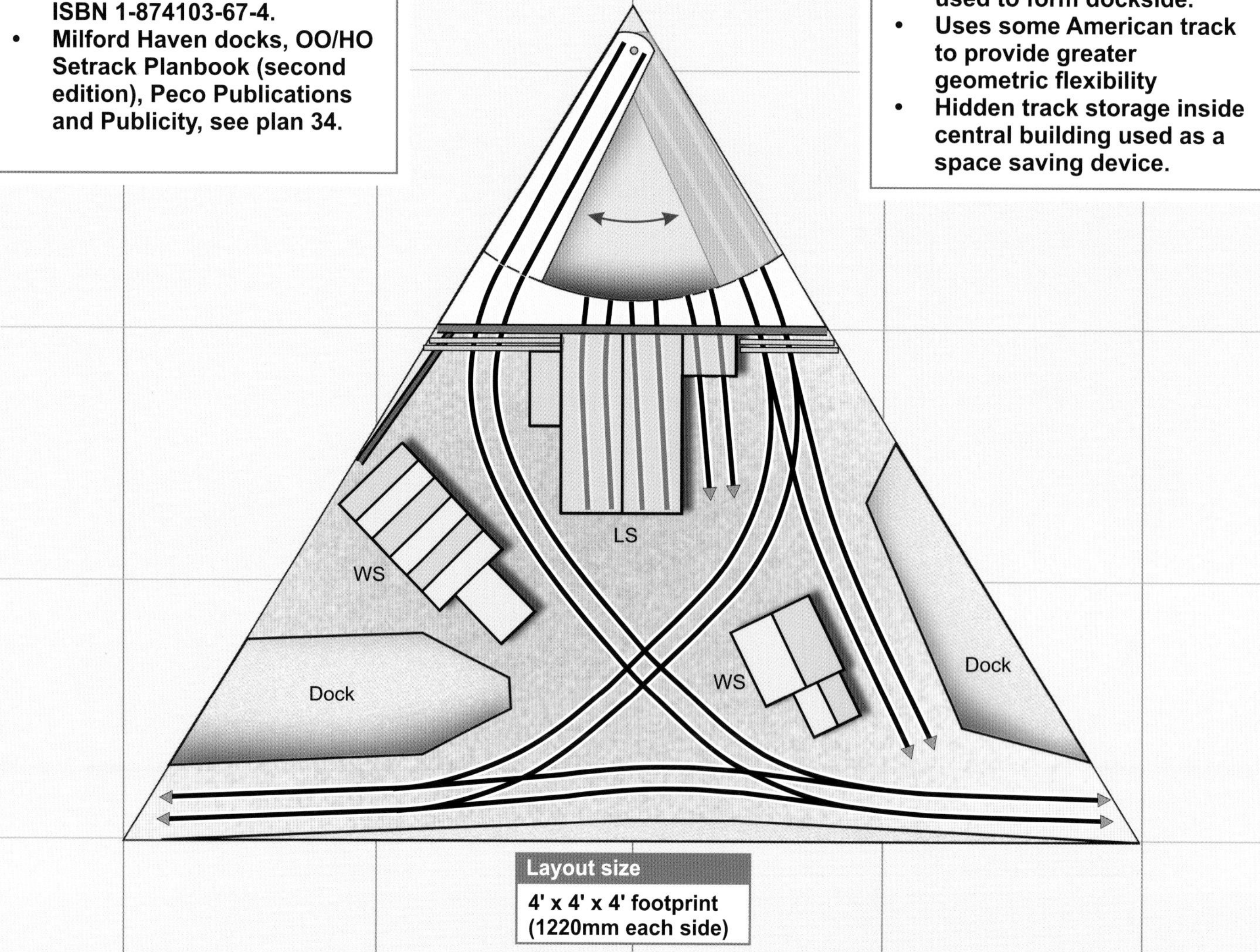

Layout size

4' x 4' x 4' footprint (1220mm each side)

Most of the dock railways I've surveyed have certain things in common; short shunting locos and wagons, extremely tight curves, diamond crossings and a plethora of buildings, one layer after another, shoe-horned into a relatively tight space. Yes, it sounds just like a micro-layout and of course it usually was. This view of Falmouth docks from 1988 has much to endear it with just the bow ends of two dry docks view blocked by buildings in the right foreground. A mandatory pair of diamond crossings is barely visible centre left and a solitary Sentinel shunter waits for the next job. There's a rich mix between old and new, and the colour scheme is fairly well balanced save for the bright whites bottom right quarter.

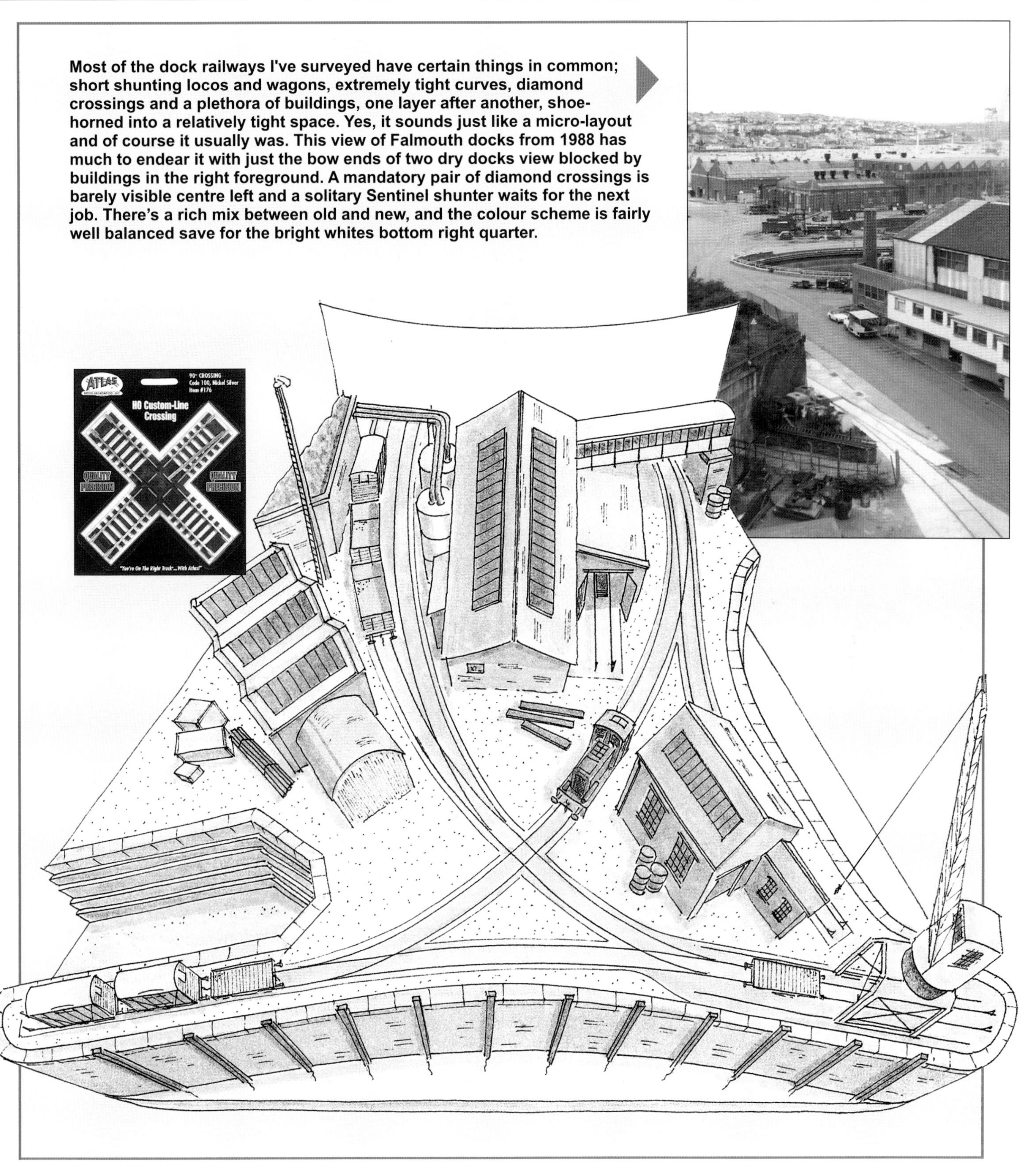

Micro Circuit

The absolute minimum continuous run

Here is a design that I believe pushes the parameters of what constitutes a micro layout. As far as a circle is concerned, save for some continental/American track or custom made curves, this is about as small as you can go and therefore, from my point of view, as a micro-layout it's definitely *in* (I'm already waiting for the letters!).

Of at least equal importance is that this is designed especially for an adult and child: recognising the central area of the layout can be quite intricate away from young and sometimes clumsy hands, whereas the outer circuit, ideal to watch trains go by, is made up of basic scenery from durable materials like lichen.

Of note, as seen in the artist's impression, is the J94 on the three sidings in contrast with items from the Thomas® range in industrial guise on a through train.

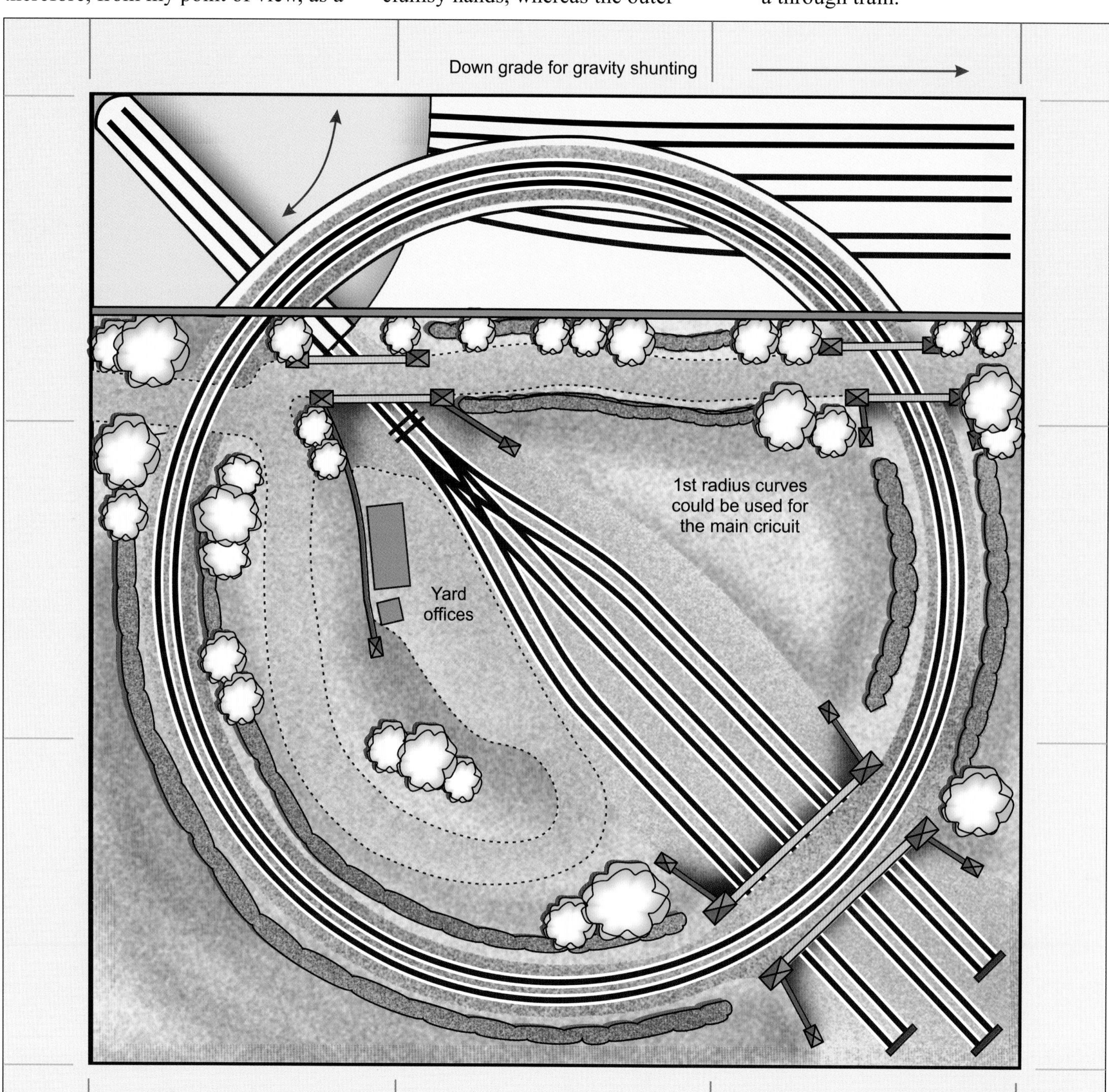

Layout size

3' x 3'
(915mm x 915mm)

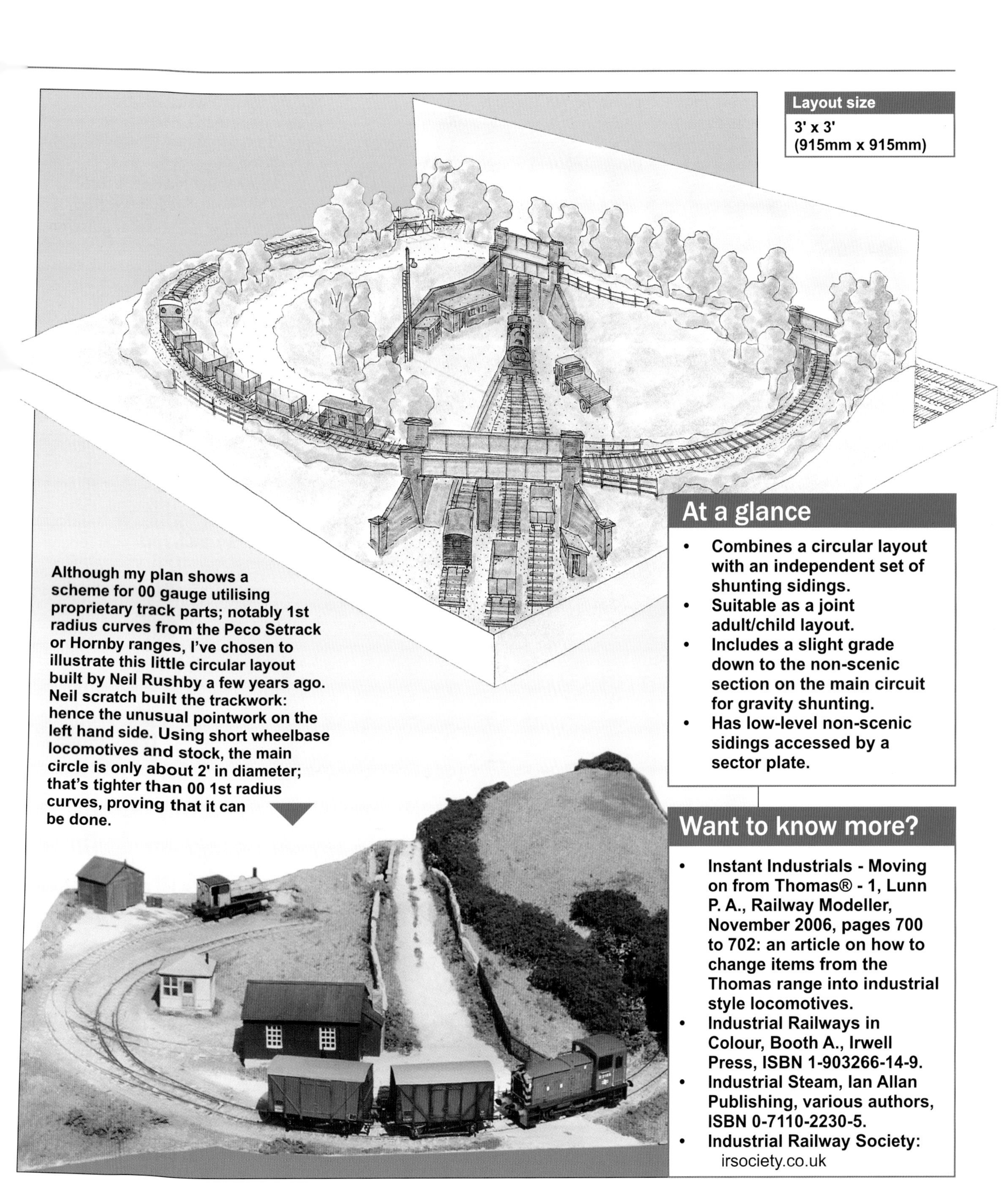

Although my plan shows a scheme for 00 gauge utilising proprietary track parts; notably 1st radius curves from the Peco Setrack or Hornby ranges, I've chosen to illustrate this little circular layout built by Neil Rushby a few years ago. Neil scratch built the trackwork: hence the unusual pointwork on the left hand side. Using short wheelbase locomotives and stock, the main circle is only about 2' in diameter; that's tighter than 00 1st radius curves, proving that it can be done.

At a glance

- Combines a circular layout with an independent set of shunting sidings.
- Suitable as a joint adult/child layout.
- Includes a slight grade down to the non-scenic section on the main circuit for gravity shunting.
- Has low-level non-scenic sidings accessed by a sector plate.

Want to know more?

- Instant Industrials - Moving on from Thomas® - 1, Lunn P. A., Railway Modeller, November 2006, pages 700 to 702: an article on how to change items from the Thomas range into industrial style locomotives.
- Industrial Railways in Colour, Booth A., Irwell Press, ISBN 1-903266-14-9.
- Industrial Steam, Ian Allan Publishing, various authors, ISBN 0-7110-2230-5.
- Industrial Railway Society: irsociety.co.uk

Layout Turntable

A rotating scene that gives ever changing views

In the absence of a revolving turntable, railway companies could always turn locos round at a triangular junction. Like Queensbury and Outwood in Yorkshire, they were always great places to watch trains because of all the stopping and starting, not to mention a surfeit of signal boxes controlling the movements. Even then, as a modeller, I think I always saw them as inside out circuits, not as fast as a circle of track, but every bit as interesting. This design can be as simple or as complicated as you'd like to make it. As drawn the layout is a self contained unit featuring the Dapol Park Royal and Silver Fox AC diesel railbuses both of which are short enough to navigate all sides of the triangle together with some modest shunting on one side.

Alternatively, have a traverser/cassette that's fixed for operating sessions, minimum length of 2', at A and you increase capacity both for shunting and for the introduction of two car DMUs into the station. Thirdly, if the whole table was made to revolve between each journey then all trains would arrive back at the main traverser/cassette. There's no denying that construction of such a facility would require a high degree of accuracy and if you're one of the faint hearted then why not go for a further option: a clip-on traverser/cassette at each of the three junctions with the table remaining fixed.

At a glance

- **Self-contained triangular junction.**
- **Layout could be displayed in a custom made circular armour glass topped table.**

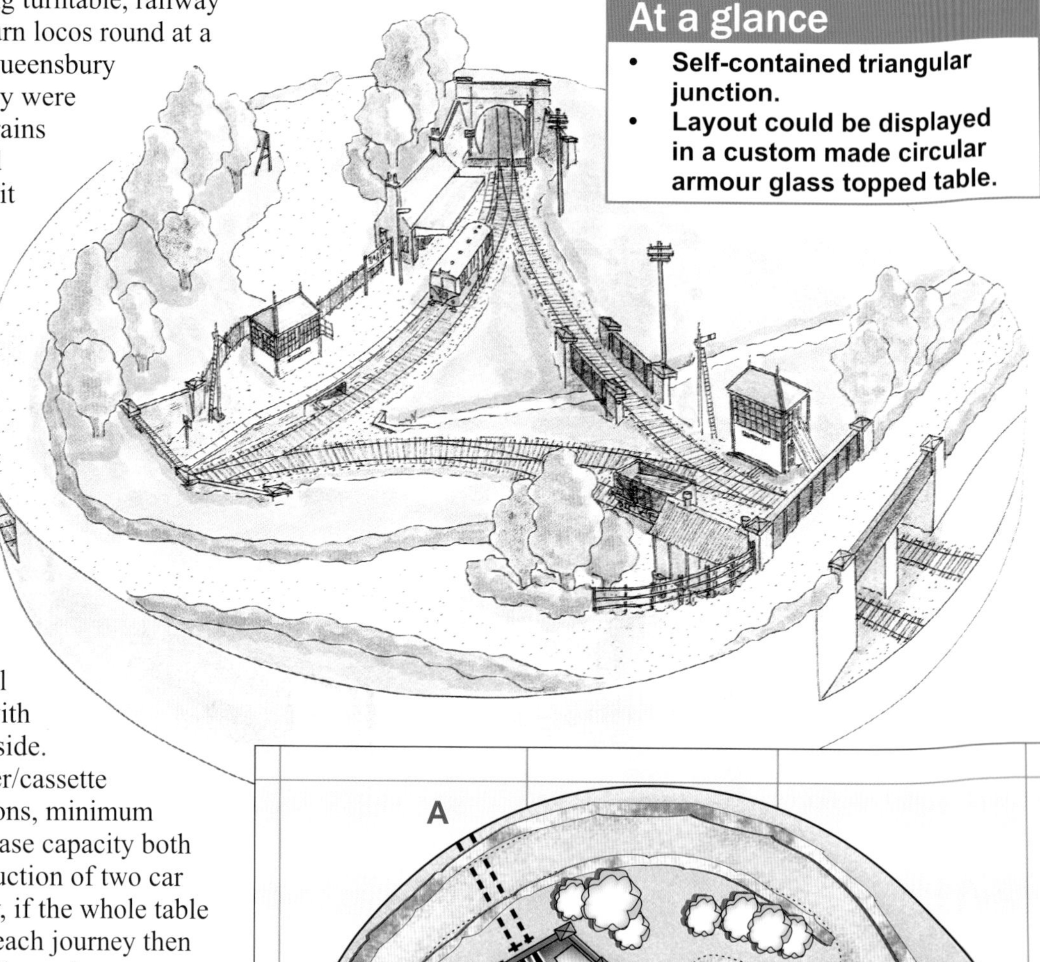

Layout size

3' diameter (915mm diameter)

Want to know more

- **The Qeensbury Lines, Whitaker A. and Cryer B. Dalesman Books, ISBN 0-85206-807-7. Photograph of the triangular station formation.**
- **BR's smallest train, Model Rail, November 2002, various authors, pages 18 to 25, modelling BR railbuses.**
- **IKEA®, many DIY and furniture retailers sell a variety of circular tables. Most, if not suitable in diameter, can have an enlarged worktop added or can be increased or reduced in height to suit.**